T0271407

ROUTLEDGE LIBRARY EDITIONS:
AGRIBUSINESS AND LAND USE

Volume 21

INDIGENOUS AGRICULTURAL REVOLUTION

ROUTLEDGE LIBRARY EDITIONS
AGRIBUSINESS AND LANDUSE

Volume 2

IN CONTROL'S
AGRICULTURAL
REVOLUTION

INDIGENOUS
AGRICULTURAL
REVOLUTION

Ecology and Food Production
in West Africa

PAUL RICHARDS

Routledge
Taylor & Francis Group

LONDON AND NEW YORK

First published in 1985 by Hutchinson & Co. (Publishers) Ltd

This edition first published in 2024
by Routledge
4 Park Square, Milton Park, Abingdon, Oxon OX14 4RN

and by Routledge
605 Third Avenue, New York, NY 10158

Routledge is an imprint of the Taylor & Francis Group, an informa business

British Library Cataloguing in Publication Data
A catalogue record for this book is available from the British Library

ISBN: 978-1-032-48321-4 (Set)
ISBN: 978-1-032-46897-6 (Volume 21) (hbk)
ISBN: 978-1-032-46909-6 (Volume 21) (pbk)
ISBN: 978-1-003-38373-4 (Volume 21) (ebk)

DOI: 10.4324/9781003383734

Publisher's Note
The publisher has gone to great lengths to ensure the quality of this reprint but points out that some imperfections in the original copies may be apparent.

Disclaimer
The publisher has made every effort to trace copyright holders and would welcome correspondence from those they have been unable to trace.

Indigenous Agricultural Revolution

Ecology and food production in West Africa

Paul Richards

Hutchinson

London Melbourne Sydney Auckland Johannesburg

Hutchinson & Co. (Publishers) Ltd

An imprint of the Hutchinson Publishing Group

17–21 Conway Street, London W1P 6JD

Hutchinson Publishing Group (Australia) Pty Ltd
16–22 Church Street, Hawthorn, Melbourne, Victoria 3122

Hutchinson Group (NZ) Ltd
32–34 View Road, PO Box 40–086, Glenfield, Auckland 10

Hutchinson Group (SA) (Pty) Ltd
PO Box 337, Bergvlei 2012, South Africa

First published 1985
© Paul Richards 1985

Set in Linotype Times by Saxon Ltd., Derby.

Printed and bound in Great Britain by
Anchor Brendon Ltd, Tiptree, Essex

British Library Cataloguing in Publication Data

Richards, Paul, *1945–*
   Indigenous agricultural revolution: ecology
   and food production in West Africa.
   1. Agricultural innovations—Developing
   countries   2. Agricultural ecology—
   Developing countries
   338.1'6   S494.5.15

ISBN 0 09 161320 5 cased
     0 09 161321 3 paper

Contents

In memoriam John Ford (1910–79)

Acknowledgements

The initial stimulus to write this book came from seven years spent teaching agricultural geography in the University of Ibadan. I am most grateful for the interest and encouragement of my Ibadan colleagues: to Michael Barbour and Akin Mabogunje for the challenging intellectual climate they so successfully sustained in their department, and to my colleagues in physical geography – Colin High, 'Toye Faniran, 'Segun Areola and Julius Oguntoyinbo – for their invaluable coffee-time 'seminars' on tropical soils, vegetation and climate. Later, when at the School of Oriental & African Studies in London, I had the great good fortune to be associated with four outstanding postgraduate projects in farming systems research. My debt to the work of Dr David Atteh (University of Ilorin), Dr Michael Johnny (Njala University College), Dr John Karimu (Fourah Bay College) and Dr Emeka Uzozie (University of Nigeria, Nsukka) will be fully apparent in the following pages. When I left Ibadan in 1974 Dr David Dalby, then Director of the International African Institute, encouraged me to further develop some of the material in this book under IAI auspices in London. The association with IAI brought me in contact with the late John Ford, an Honorary Research Fellow of the Institute. John's influence on my thinking will be apparent throughout this book.

I would also like to thank other IAI colleagues – Djibril Diallo, Nicola Harris, Abdul Mejid Hussein, Phil O'Keefe and Ben Wisner – for their help and encouragement. Most recently Phil

Burnham, Murray Last and Barrie Sharpe, all of the Anthropology Department at University College London, have helped me find my bearings in the anthropological and sociological literature relating to African agriculture. Colleagues and students at Njala University College made me welcome on a year's study leave in 1982–3 and helped me reformulate a number of ideas in this book from the standpoint of the practising agriculturist. I am especially grateful to the Njala cartographer, Mr E. A. Okine, for drawing a number of the diagrams. Dr John Flinn, agricultural economist at IITA, and more recently at IRRI, has kept me informed over a number of years about the work of the International Agricultural Research Centers. The series editor, Professor Michael Crowder, Dr David Gibbon of the University of East Anglia and my UCL colleagues Kathy Homewood and Nick Maxwell made helpful comments on earlier drafts of the book (but, of course, bear no responsibility for remaining errors of fact or judgement). Nick Maxwell arranged for me to run Chapter 5 past the gauntlet of his History and Philosophy of Science seminar. Chapter 1 received equally useful improving comment from the African History seminar at the School of Oriental & African Studies. Special thanks are due to my wife and son for allowing me long periods of pencil-sucking solitude.

Paul Richards
University College London

Introduction:

science, agriculture and environment in West Africa

This book concerns the relationship between science and development – more especially the relationship between environmental science and prospects for increased food production in West Africa.

Recently, I had the opportunity to contribute to a course in environmental studies for a group of agriculture students in a West African university. Each student undertook a field project in a village in the vicinity of the campus. The objectives of the project were to describe three 'typical' farms, to provide, in scientific terms, an assessment of the way each farm was run, and after detailed discussion with the farmer, to propose technical solutions to his or her most pressing environmental management problems.

The work was well done, and the reports make fascinating reading. I think many of the students were genuinely surprised to find out how much farmers already knew about the ecological processes at work in their farms. The students had little difficulty in 'translating' this knowledge into textbook scientific terms. Some were sufficiently impressed by this knowledge to ask farmers' advice on problems they had come across in the course of experiments on the college farm.

In the end, however, it became clear that the students had learnt more from the farmers than the farmers had learnt from the students. Few textbook solutions to agricultural development problems seemed relevant or feasible given the realities of the farms described. The problems that farmers themselves listed as priorities were ones on which the textbooks remained silent. The students came back from the field not with a list of recommendations offered but an agenda of research issues upon which they would have to start work from scratch. The project had demonstrated the width of the gap between what science has to offer and the needs of typical West African small-scale farmers. The nature of this gap, what might be done about it, and what it tells us about the links between science and development, are the themes of this book.

Scientific universals and ecological particularism

Most scientists would subscribe to the view that science deals in universals: principles that are true for all times and places. They would say that it makes sense to talk of Yoruba music, Islamic art, Marxist history, but less sense to regard the laws of physics and chemistry in the same way. There are, so it would be argued, no Marxist laws of soil erosion or Yoruba principles of rainfall. Science derives its unique power to transform the world precisely because it is not confined to the particularities of time, place and special interests.

One of the justifications once advanced in favour of colonialism was that it brought Africa under the 'rule of law'. This was meant, I think, in two senses. First that British or French principles of jurisprudence were beneficial to Africa because they were based on 'universal' notions of human rights, and second, that colonialism connected Africa to the global march of progress by bringing scientific principles to bear on development problems.

The first argument has been widely, and rightly, contested. If there are universal principles of jurisprudence these are not located in the surface layers of legal systems, but by analogy with a term used by linguists, in their 'deep structures'. Looked at in this light there are as many universals in African law as in European. Assessed at the level of 'deep structure' it would be difficult to claim the innate superiority of European legal codes over African. At the surface level, European codes were often quite manifestly unsuited to African conditions.

Would a similar argument be true of the sciences? Did colonial scientific and technical departments see themselves as bringing the 'anarchy' of the African environment under the rule of scientific law? And were these laws as beneficial as their protagonists hoped?

John Ford (1971),* surveying the lessons to be learnt from attempts by the colonial scientific services to solve the 'tsetse fly problem', argues that inflexible commitment to universalist assumptions of this sort fundamentally misdirected trypanosomiasis research for a generation or more. Drawing on many years of

*Full references quoted in the text are contained in the Bibliography beginning on p.173.

experience as an entomologist working for the colonial sleeping sickness services, Ford arrived at the conclusion that the spread of tsetse flies and sleeping sickness in the early colonial period was a direct consequence of disruptions brought about by colonial conquest. Colonial administrators found it difficult to appreciate that they themselves were partly the cause of the problem they were struggling to solve. So the erroneous idea became firmly established that the spread of the tsetse fly hazard was due to the 'outmoded' and 'wasteful' cultivation practices of African farmers.

African environmental management practices reflected sets of conditions and constraints with which scientists trained in Europe were unfamiliar. Africa was a lightly populated continent. Many of the key issues in the ecology of development derived from the zone of contact between the wilderness and the settled domain. The African trypanosomiases, Ford argues, were characteristic of the diseases that have to be overcome when settlements and wildlife ecosystems come into contact. French, Belgian and British scientists in Africa came from densely-settled countries where the problem of 'wilderness diseases' had been overcome many centuries earlier. Many African communities, however, were still engaged upon the work of taming the wilderness at the time of colonial conquest, in part due to depopulation caused by earlier contact with Europe (notably the slave trade, cf. Inikori, 1982). Russian ecologists, confronting the problems posed by a major wilderness settlement frontier in Siberia, had elaborated theories much more relevant to African conditions (so Ford argues), but Russia was never a colonial power in Africa. French, Belgian and British colonialists, convinced of their own intellectual and cultural superiority, failed to understand both how particular and place-bound were their own principles of environmental resource management, and the extent to which many of the characteristic practices of African farmers and pastoralists were effective responses to the highly specific challenges posed by the African environment.

After several decades of failure to control the trypanosomiasis problem in colonial Africa scientists eventually concluded that many of their 'solutions' made the problem worse and not better, and that it might be advisable to reassess indigenous management strategies. Ford concludes by reversing previous judgements. Far from being a cause of the tsetse problem, African farming methods offered many useful pointers to an effective solution. Ford's study (which I return to in greater detail in Chapter 5) suggests, therefore, that especial attention should be paid to the particularities of ecological relationships in the African environment. This is not to dismiss universals in the ecological sciences altogether. Still less is it support for the notion that science is 'a central villain in the exhaustion and despoliation of man's own environment' (Ley & Samuel, 1978: 1). What Ford's work suggests, however, is that in ecological and agricultural studies the universals often lie on deeper levels than hitherto has been suspected.

The present book is written with some of the lessons of John Ford's study in mind. The main argument may be summed up as follows. Intellectuals, development agencies and governments have all pursued environmental management problems at too high a level of abstraction and generalization. Many environmental problems are, in fact, localized and specific, and require local, ecologically particular, responses. The issue then becomes how to stimulate such situation-specific responses. One of the answers explored below is through mobilizing and building upon existing local skills and initiatives. Everything should be done – so the argument runs – to stimulate vigorous 'indigenous science' and 'indigenous technology'.

The book is addressed to those interested in the role of environmental sciences in development, more especially those whose work requires them to translate general principles of environmental resource management into practical advice directly relevant to the needs of West African small-holders. Special attention is paid to ways of ensuring that agricultural research and extension is adequately flexible and responsive to local needs. Proposals are considered for strengthening local research and problem-solving capacities. Particular stress is laid on the importance of involving farmers directly in the formulation of research agenda, and on their active participation in the research process itself.

Illustrating the case for 'ecological particularism' requires me to deal primarily in case-study material; hence a concentration on specific instances, mainly drawn from fieldwork in Nigeria and Sierra Leone. The argument of the book, however, is relevant to a wider audience than those with a special interest in West Africa. Similar approaches to those advocated here are being pursued in other tropical and sub-tropical regions (cf. Biggs & Clay, 1981; Brokensha, Warren & Werner, 1980; Chambers, 1983; Compton, 1984; Gupta, 1984; Warren, 1984). A number of these studies share a common interest in the methodological issues raised by ecological particularism. Perhaps the most significant of these is how to avoid glib generalization concerning environmental and agro-ecological issues (of a kind often apparent in journalistic accounts of African famine, and, less excusably, in some recent debates on the 'political economy' of tropical agricultural development) without collapsing into *ad hoc* arguments and special pleading. It is this, then, that constitutes the issue of general interest in the present book: how to throw away the dirty bathwater of 'Grand Theory' in tropical ecological sciences without at the same time losing grip of the slippery baby of situation-specific, development-relevant, environmental understanding.

The steps in the argument

Subsequent to this introduction, the book is divided into six chapters.

Chapter 1 is a critical examination of agricultural research and development policies and related issues of environmental management in the colonial period. The failure of a number of early initiatives taught an important lesson: the West African environment posed a specific set of challenges well understood by farmers within the region, but less well understood by science. Little progress was made while colonial agricultural agencies thought exclusively in terms of 'technology transfer' (reliance on ideas and techniques that had proved successful in other parts of the world). Matters started to improve during the 1930s when researchers began to look closely at local cultivation practices. On the eve of the Second World War the West Africa Commission proposed a new 'ecological' approach in which farmer and scientist would pool their skills in an attempt to improve rather than replace existing farming systems.

This option was swept to one side by wartime emergencies and a new 'frontal attack' on agricultural development problems after the war. In these post-war initiatives machines rather than the skills of the small-holder were to be the cutting edge of agricultural change. But repeated failures to implement successfully large-scale mechanized cultivation under West African conditions have necessitated a reassessment of the issues involved. In consequence, the last 10–15 years has seen a renewed focus of interest on small-holder farming systems. This has been part of a global re-evaluation of the skills of the peasant farmer as 'the single largest resource not yet mobilized in the development enterprise' (Chambers, 1983).

The ecological basis for the argument that peasant enterprise has already laid the foundations for an agricultural revolution in West Africa is examined in Chapters 2-4. Chapters 2 and 3 consider some of the more important ecological principles exploited by small-holder farming systems in West Africa. The evidence suggests that small-holder environmental management is dynamic and innovative, and not merely 'adaptive'. This is not to argue that 'peasant agriculture' needs no inputs or assistance from the formal research sector, but to point out that a thorough ecological understanding of the aims and methods of small-scale producers is necessary if inputs from scientific research and the development agencies are to complement and augment local trends and interests. The history of formal-sector interventions in West Africa is that many have proved irrelevant or harmful, even when aimed directly at small-holders, because of a failure to assess local interests in advance. Two detailed examples of change and invention in West African food production systems – one a case where population densities are low, the other where they are high – are discussed in Chapter 4. Both cases are examples of effective exploitation of highly specific configurations of environmental resources and of local capacities for innovation in the face of changing ecological and economic circumstances.

It sometimes appears that invention and ecological adaptation in African agriculture are at their most vigorous where external agencies have interfered least. This paradox is addressed in Chapter 5. If it is indeed the case that scientific agriculture and agricultural development agencies have sometimes done more harm than good, why has this situation arisen and what can be done about it? It is relevant to look at the way agricultural research and development (R & D) is organized. A tendency towards centralization of resources, preference for 'universal' explanation, and a belief in science as the 'cutting edge' of technological transformation all pose problems in the African context. These points are illustrated by reference to Ford's account of colonial attempts to rid Africa of the 'tsetse menace', and more recent attempts to promote an African 'Green Revolution'.

The book concludes with a chapter outlining an alternative model for the relationship between science and development. A case is argued for 'people's science'; a decentralized, participatory, R & D system which seeks to support, rather than replace, local initiative.

People's science and agrarian populism

The notion of 'people's science' relates to a broader set of arguments about agricultural change sometimes termed 'agrarian populism'. It would be appropriate to round out this introduction by noting some of the ideas and experiences denoted by this term.

Debates concerning agrarian populism were important among Russian socialists in the late nineteenth century. In contradistinction to the views of many orthodox Marxists, the populists rejected 'evolutionist' interpretations of agrarian change, arguing instead that it would be possible to pass from feudalism to socialism without capitalist agriculture as an intervening 'stage' (Walicki, 1969; Kofi, 1980). Translated into action, the populist approach sought to transform Russian agriculture through appeal to peasant economic interests and cultural values, and through the improvement of existing peasant institutions and systems of production.

After the revolution the agricultural economist Chayanov developed an influential theory of peasant economy, derived from detailed studies of peasant farming systems, in which emphasis was placed on both the durability of the peasantry as a social grouping and the 'non-capitalist' rationality of many peasant decision-making procedures. These notions ran contrary to the Leninist argument that the peasantry was undergoing rapid differentiation into a class of capitalist farmers and a mass of landless labourers (cf. Lenin, 1899). A pro-peasant development programme was worked out in practical detail by Chayanov and colleagues during the 1920s (Harrison, 1981). Further experiments on populist lines, however, were terminated by the drive towards collectivization and 'industrial' methods of production in Soviet agriculture under Stalin.

Populism was also a significant force in late nineteenth-century agriculture in the United States (Hofstadter, 1969). Whereas Russian agrarian populism was an intellectual programme in support of the peasantry, American populism was a political movement (directed in particular against urban-based financial speculators) organized by small and medium-scale farmers themselves. Populism was a strong force among 'family farmers' in the cotton belt and the prairie wheat lands, many of whom, despite a fine record for commercial and technical enterprise, found themselves threatened by especially poor prices and high credit charges during the last quarter of the nineteenth century.

In addition to the direct political significance of American populism (e.g. the activities of the Popular Party in the 1890s) populist attitudes had a profound influence on educational and agricultural research institutions. In some measure, both the Land Grant College movement, and the organization of state agricultural extension services came to reflect this populist heritage. American extension agents were seen, initially, as employees of the farming community, not agents of a centralized scientific bureaucracy (in many countries – in Britain for example – extension workers are counted as civil servants, with the implication that their loyalty lies to the state not the farming community). A priority for a number of early extension services in the United States was to communicate farmers' needs to researchers, not to disseminate scientific findings to potential users. Under a populist rubric extension workers were truly 'agents' (professionals charged with the representation of their clients' interests) rather than the 'educators', 'communicators', even 'salesmen', they have since become.

In Africa, the term populism has been used to describe peasant resistance movements directed against colonial and capitalist penetration and to characterize a number of idioms of 'nationalist' politics (Kilson, 1967; Saul, 1969; Worsley, 1969). The term has also been used in a programmatic sense as a rallying call for pro-rural, pro-peasant, development strategies (Fanon, 1968; Kofi, 1980; Williams, 1976). A revived interest in agrarian populism in this second sense reflects the depth of the current food-production crisis in Africa, and the apparent ineffectiveness of orthodox initiatives for dealing with this problem.

The present book draws much of its inspiration from populist arguments of the following kinds:

1 Whereas much of Africa's rural population is scattered and poor it is also inventively self-reliant. The degree of isolation and poverty is in many cases such as to foredoom to failure attempts to copy agricultural development strategies attempted in Europe and Asia. On the other hand, inventive self-reliance is one of Africa's most precious resources. Development initiatives should aim to maximize the utilization of this resource.

2 Small-scale farmers are capable of making changes in their own interest which are potentially of benefit to society as a whole.

The most effective and rapid rates of agricultural change will occur when state resources are used to back changes that small-scale farmers are already keen to make. (Such support will not be applied indiscriminately to all peasant interests, of course, but will inevitably reflect wider societal goals and priorities.)

3   Although rural development programmes of the last 10–15 years have placed the interests of small-scale farmers high on their agenda, the results have so far failed to come up to expectations because of a failure seriously to address questions of popular participation in project design and the development of new technologies. This results either in inappropriate innovations or in support for the least appropriate groups in the farming community. Typically, project inputs fail to work as intended or they end up in the hands of non-farmers (merchants, transporters, civil servants, politicians) and those most anxious to quit farming for town.

I must stress, however, that the politics, sociology and economics of agrarian populism are not my main concern in this book. These are issues dealt with effectively elsewhere (Chambers, 1983; Harriss, 1983; Ionescu & Gellner, 1969; Williams, 1976). My main concern is with ecological aspects of the populist case; more specifically, with the possibility that the populist approach is a good, and perhaps the most effective, way to foster the resource-management and biological skills upon which an African agricultural revolution might rest.

1 Food crops and environment:
colonial policy and present dilemmas

What kinds of agricultural development and resource management policies have already been tried in West Africa? What lessons relevant to current difficulties might be learnt from a consideration of earlier policy initiatives? This chapter attempts to answer these questions by a consideration of the history of colonial agricultural research and development (R & D) policies in anglophone West Africa. Some of the general arguments are illustrated by reference to specific experience in one country – Sierra Leone.

Early policy debates

Botanical gardens were the focus of initial efforts by colonial administrations to make an input into agriculture. These gardens – e.g. those at Ebute Meta near Lagos and at Calabar – were connected to an Empire-wide network for the exchange of planting materials, co-ordinated by the Royal Botanical Gardens at Kew (Brockway, 1979). Colonial botanical gardens were intended to facilitate the transfer of new or improved cash crops to chiefs, traders and wealthier peasant farmers interested in establishing small plantations. A number of studies have shown conclusively, however, that these official efforts were marginal rather than central to the development of cash-crop production in the early colonial period.

The major nineteenth-century expansion of groundnut production in Senegal and oil palm production in Sierra Leone and eastern Nigeria, and the later development of cocoa in Ghana, Ivory Coast and western Nigeria, and of groundnut cultivation in northern Nigeria, depended almost entirely on indigenous initiatives (Berry, 1975; Crowder, 1982; Hill, 1963; Hogendorn, 1978). In a number of cases this applied even to the first introduction of exotic planting materials and techniques. Cocoa was introduced to Ghana by a migrant returning home from Fernando Po, and Yoruba freed slaves returning to Lagos from Brazil introduced the technique for making the type of cassava meal known as *gari*. This latter was one of the most important innovations in African food-producing techniques in the nineteenth century, since it permitted the widespread cultivation of high-yielding 'bitter' varieties of cassava, hitherto unfit for human consumption because of a high content of hydrocyanic acid (Agboola, 1968).

Government initiative had greater impact in the field of forest conservation. Most parts of the forest zone in West Africa witnessed a major boom in the exploitation of timber and wild rubber (e.g. *Landolphia heudelotii*) during the 1890s. Slaughter tapping of rubber was practised on a wide scale, and officials feared for the future of the trade (correctly, as it turned out). The issue of tapping licences, prosecution in cases of unauthorized forest exploitation, and delimitation of 'reserved' forests were important, even dominant, aspects of the colonial administrative presence in a number of districts.

In more settled economic conditions from 1900 onwards attention began to be given to questions of agricultural research and extension. Up until 1920 the policy of Departments of Agriculture in British West Africa was based on what Sampson & Crowther (1943) term the Caribbean Model: concentration on export cash crops with little or no thought for indigenous food supply.

In 1920, an agriculturalist with Indian experience, O.T. Faulkner, was appointed as Director of the Nigerian Department of Agriculture (the largest, and therefore potentially the most influential, such department in British West Africa). According to Sampson & Crowther (1943), Indian departments of agriculture had been forced, by widespread famine conditions during the nineteenth century, to place a greater emphasis on peasant farmer food crops and farming systems. They trace a similar change in emphasis in Nigeria to Faulkner's influence.

A number of factors in the period prior to Faulkner's arrival served to underline the wisdom of a shift from the Caribbean to the Indian policy model. Three experiences might be cited as illustrations:

1   Clear evidence of small-holder capacity for rapid agricultural change in the first great wave of expansion in the cocoa belt of

western Nigeria (Berry, 1975) and the opening up of groundnut cultivation in northern Nigeria (Hogendorn, 1978).

2   A major famine in northern Nigeria, not unconnected with the shift of resources into groundnut cultivation (Shenton & Watts, 1979; Watts, 1983).

3   Failure to establish American Allen long-staple cotton as a cash crop in northern Nigeria – an object lesson in some of the pitfalls of 'external' interventions in the agricultural sector.

About the time of Faulkner's appointment, Lever Brothers' attempts (begun in 1907) to acquire land for oil-palm plantations in Nigeria were finally rebuffed by the Governor, Sir Hugh Clifford. Clifford argued that peasant farmers had proved adequately adaptable to market demands for export crops, and that alienation of land on a large scale to European business interests threatened insurmountable political difficulties (Hopkins, 1973). Subsequently, part of the task of the Department of Agriculture was to elaborate R & D policies supportive of the pro-peasant alternative. The approach adopted embraced food-crop production as well as cash and tree crops. Faulkner was suspicious of offering farmers untried innovations, and argued for a long-term approach, with a heavy emphasis on research station experimentation in the first instance (White, 1981).

'Shifting cultivation' was a major focus of this research. Faulkner was not as unreflectingly hostile to shifting cultivation as many other colonial agriculturalists of his generation. (Much of this hostility was, in fact, derivative of earlier forest conservation concerns.) He recognized that in areas where land was still abundant the system could be considered rational, efficient and stable; a viewpoint summed up in his advocacy of the non-pejorative term 'rotational bush fallowing' to describe the kind of shifting cultivation most commonly met with in southern Nigeria (Faulkner & Mackie, 1933).

Under Faulkner, and his successor Mackie, the Nigerian Department of Agriculture thus pursued a gradualist policy towards the improvement of rotational fallow farming. Careful research was needed to understand thoroughly how such farming systems operated, and to ascertain viable alternatives to the restoration or maintenance of soil fertility via bush fallowing. In southern, forested, districts the major emphasis was placed on a series of experiments with green manures and planted fallows. In northern

Nigeria, interest centred on attempts to introduce a system of 'mixed farming' involving ox ploughing.

Policy and practice: lessons from Sierra Leone

A thousand miles to the west, in Sierra Leone, colonial agricultural policy underwent a broadly similar sequence of developments to that in Nigeria. Here, a primary concern for forest conservation was, perhaps, even stronger than in Nigeria. A small agriculture department was established in up-country headquarters at Njala as early as 1912, but in 1920 the department was brought under the overall control of the Chief Conservator of Lands and Forests, M.T. Dawe. Most of the Sierra Leone administration's revenue derived from taxes on exports of palm produce. The bulk of palm produce came from self-seeded palms in forest regrowth. The administration was especially sensitive to the dangers posed by undue population pressure on forest fallows. Palms were often accidentally damaged when felled vegetation on adjacent upland rice farms was burned. A prime aim of policy was to ensure that the history of rapid decline in exports of camwood and wild rubber, due to over-exploitation in the late nineteenth century, was not repeated in the case of palm produce exports.

Dawe and his colleagues came to the conclusion that the best way to conserve palm bush, and Sierra Leone's reserves of export timber, was to try and dissuade farmers from growing upland rice altogether. This was the beginning of a single-minded emphasis on promoting swamp rice cultivation that continues to this day (see below).

Faulkner's balanced appreciation of the merits as well as demerits of shifting cultivation took longer to become established in Sierra Leone for two main reasons – the importance of oil palms as Sierra Leone's major export, and the fact that the crop was gathered rather than planted, which in the eyes of colonial policy makers made it more vulnerable to pressure from the 'unwise' land-use practices of subsistence cultivators.

Nevertheless, by the 1940s the Faulkner view was beginning to win some acceptance. The 1948 Annual Report of the Agriculture Department notes the judgement in Lord Hailey's *African Survey* (1938:1) that shifting cultivation was less a device of barbarism and more a concession to the nature of Africa's soils. Hailey's judgement itself owed much to a dissenting section, on Nigeria, in a chapter of the *Survey* devoted to soil management problems. This chapter was mainly the work of Elspeth Huxley, and it embodied a new-found world-wide concern for soil conservation, arising in particular from the experience of 'dust bowl' conditions in the United States (Jacks & Whyte, 1939). The Nigerian section of this chapter (clearly reflecting Faulkner's views on shifting cultivation) exempted Nigerian peasant farmers from the general charge of mismanagement commonly levied against the farming community by environmentalists in the 1930s:

Erosion in the Southern Provinces is to a large extent controlled by the traditional native system of cultivation, which is to grow crops on mounds made by throwing up the top layer of soil, so as to bury the weeds and grass; in addition mixed cropping is practised, so that the land is rarely left without vegetal cover. Investigation has shown this system to be sound, and the policy of the Agricultural Department is to foster it... (Hailey, 1938:1103).

The geographer L. Dudley Stamp went even further, arguing that soil conservation techniques practised by peasant farmers in northern Nigeria were so sensible that they might well become a model for farmers in more 'developed' parts of the world (Stamp, 1938).

The Sierra Leone 1948 Annual Report continues:

Any reform of shifting cultivation, *if reform is necessary*, may involve the obligation to persuade the native farmer to modify his methods of farming... It would therefore appear most necessary to first understand the underlying principles of traditional African farming practices before attempting to impose new and alternative (and possibly not well tried) methods on a conservative people (p.33: my emphasis).

The Njala soil scientist, H.W. Dougall, had embarked on a series of experiments to determine the precise merits and demerits of bush burning, perhaps the most controversial aspect of upland shifting cultivation in Sierra Leone. Dougall demonstrated that *in situ* burning of brushed vegetation (the local practice on upland rice farms) gave much the highest yields and least weed growth of three treatments tried (Table 1).

This new approach, if due partly to Faulkner's influence, also reflected the lessons of earlier policy interventions within Sierra Leone. Undeterred by previous failures, the Department of Agriculture tried, in 1923, to promote production of Sierra Leone cotton for export. A bulk order was placed in Nigeria for improved seed (Allen long-staple), with the intention of distributing this seed

Table 1 *Data on bush-burning experiments at Njala*

Treatment	Rice yield[†] (lb/acre)	Grain/straw ratio	Soil pH*	Exchangeable bases (mg E/100g)*
Vegetation burnt in situ	886	0.43	5.9	11.7
Remove vegetation for burning, return ash to farm	327	0.41	5.4	9.75
Farm brushed and all vegetation removed from farm (no burning)	199	0.29	5.2	8.78

[†] Rice variety: **bologuti**, 60 lb/acre, broadcast 25 May.
* Soils sampled post-harvest.

Source: Annual Report for 1948, Sierra Leone Department of Agriculture.

to peasant farmers throughout the country. The department also prepared a pamphlet, with the confident title *An ABC on Cotton Growing in Sierra Leone*, advising farmers on 'correct' cultivation procedures.

The pamphlet in question notes that three local varieties of cotton are already cultivated (listing their names in Mende), but condemns local cultivation practices. Cotton was grown exclusively as an intercrop on upland rice farms. This, it was said (but with little evidence?) 'only keeps alive various cotton pests'. Departmental policy was against anything that encouraged upland rice. The main argument, however, against local techniques of cotton cultivation (implied rather than stated) was that West African short-staple varieties were of little interest to Lancashire manufacturers. Conversely, the exotic varieties of greatest value on the export market were ill-adapted to intercropping.

Thus farmers were exhorted to make separate farms for cotton because only this would allow them to grow 'cotton of the best kind' for which (the pamphlet asserts) 'there will always be a market in Europe' and 'the future price will be high.' Farmers are advised to clear and stump their cotton farms – advice that reads a little strangely in relation to contemporary heated condemnation of upland rice cultivation for exposing fragile soils to the eroding impact of Sierra Leone's intense and heavy rainfall. Douglas Scotland, the author of the pamphlet, suggests farmers make transverse ridges to minimize the erosion problem, but offers no advice on how this is to be done in circumstances where most farmers were already short of labour.

A subsequent pamphlet, *Report on recent attempts to establish the cultivation of cotton in Sierra Leone* (1926), details an almost complete fiasco. When difficulties first became apparent, some comparative trials were undertaken. The nearest these trials came to success was with a local variety, **kwande**, but 'local demand for making country cloths was sufficiently great to absorb a fair amount of the cotton produced' (pp. 2-3). No wonder, since the export price was only 25 per cent of the local price!

In writing the second pamphlet, Scotland was moved to ask 'a natural question...why try out exotic cottons when we have suitable indigenous ones to work upon?' His own view was that local varieties could only rarely be improved beyond a certain point and that it was, in any case, difficult ever to get hold of pure seed. This he blamed on 'the native custom of mixed cropping', in which 'sowing is very indiscriminate' with 'no seed selection...with the result that one cannot call **kwande** a cultivated type' (p.14). Others of his staff, however, had begun to consider whether there might be some important lessons to be learnt from local agricultural practices. J.V.R. Brown, Superintendent of Agriculture for Central Province, while speculating that Allen cotton was ill-adapted to intercropping with rice, wondered nevertheless whether such an approach might not be a success 'from the point of view of freedom from insect attack' (p.6). Modern research confirms that intercropping is sometimes highly beneficial as a pest control strategy (Ajibola Taylor, 1977; Steiner, 1982).

The lessons of the cotton fiasco were equally relevant to rice. Up until 1919 the colonial administration in Sierra Leone (as indeed throughout most of tropical Africa) had given little thought to questions of food crop farming. The influenza pandemic known in Europe as the 'Spanish Lady' reached Sierra Leone in August–September 1918. So serious was its impact on up-country farming communities just prior to the harvest season that it is estimated that the rice harvest was reduced to 50–60 per cent of its normal level. As a result, Freetown, swollen by its wartime workforce, experienced serious food shortages in mid-1919. Hostility was directed against the Lebanese trading community, suspected of hoarding rice, and of shipping it back up country out of the reach of government price controls. The government dithered, and serious rioting broke out in July (Spitzer, 1975).

Early in 1920 the Governor of Sierra Leone – with the riots fresh in mind – suggested to the Secretary of State for the Colonies the idea of obtaining the services of an expert to advise on irrigated rice cultivation. It was thought that the time was not ripe for a 'highly qualified technical expert to prepare a general scheme for the development of the cultivation of irrigated rice' but that it might be more appropriate to arrange 'some elementary practical instruction [for] the native rice growers' (Colonial Annual Report for 1922).

This patronizing proposal received its just deserts when A.C. Pillai, an Indian agriculturalist asked to advise on rice cultivation in the mangrove swamps of the estuaries of the Scarcies Rivers, reported that yields obtained by Temne farmers were better than the average for Madras (Table 2), and that there was little if anything that he could advise that farmers did not already know and practice. Asked about development of rice cultivation in the Sherbro Estuary, where farmers were less experienced in cultivating mangrove swamps, Pillai thought it might be best simply to

Table 2 *Scarcies and Madras rice yields compared*

	Yield (clean rice, lb/acre)		Yield (clean rice, lb/acre)
Madras Presidency		*Sierra Leone*	
Godavery Delta	1007	Scarcies	1434*
Kristna	1010		
Trichinopoly	1316		
Madras	1458		
Tinnevelly	1448		

* Figures in original table 1343 lb but given as 1434 lb in text.

Source: Colonial reports: report for 1922 (no. 1165), London: HMSO, 1923.

invite experienced farmers from the Scarcies region to carry out
relevant extension work.

Pillai's findings and advice elicited a truculent response from the
Colonial Administration:

In other words, in spite of careless and negligent cultivation the yield is as
good as that of the good deltaic lands in India, the reason being that there
are in Sierra Leone immense natural facilities for procuring good crops
(Colonial Annual Report for 1922, p.21).

It took some time, and, more specifically, a careful survey of local
farming practices in the Scarcies region by Glanville, the agricultural officer for the Northern Province, before the message sank in.
Glanville's survey scotched the idea that the good yields achieved
by Temne farmers in the Scarcies were happy accidents of nature.
These farmers obtained good yields because they knew what they
were doing. Furthermore, as reports based on Glanville's survey
demonstrate (Glanville, 1933; 1938), this was not a question of
'traditions' refined by a long process of trial and error and handed
down from generation to generation, but of active innovation and
invention by local farmers in the recent past.

Techniques for cultivating mangrove swamps – derived, perhaps,
from practices of farmers further along the Upper Guinea coast
(Harrison Church, 1974; Rodney, 1970) – had first been im-
plemented in the latter half of the nineteenth century, largely in
response to the stimulus provided by the Freetown market.
According to Glanville (1938) 'in or about 1885...', after some years
in which farmers had occasionally broadcast rice in tidal sedge lands
behind the mangrove 'one man had the initiative to experiment in
the mangrove swamp, which had the advantage of comparative
freedom from weed growth. He was so successful that others
followed his example...' and the region rapidly became the major
supplier of rice to the expanding Freetown market.

Glanville is especially insistent that a number of crucial innovations were local discoveries. To begin with seed was pre-germinated
and broadcast, but because of the tides this gave irregular results
and transplanting was soon adopted. He offers two possible
explanations of the origins of transplanting: that farmers developed
the idea from the experience of taking seedlings from upland farms
to fill in gaps on the swamp, or that the technique was introduced
from Guinea, where the Temne had gone to help the Susu in war.
He adds that '...Temne farmers soon...devised an improvement

[for planting, to replace the pointed stick dibbler] in the forked transplanting instrument which inserted the seedlings direct'. An alternative to Douglas Scotland's dim view of local skills in varietal selection is then propounded: 'the Scarcies farmer is always on the look out for anything new in the rice line and is undoubtedly responsible for propagating several new varieties from field selections'.

In his 1938 report Glanville points out that local initiative was not confined to mangrove swamps alone, but had been responsible for the development of swamp rice cultivation in inland valley swamps as a complement to upland cultivation. At a number of points Glanville tempers a 'textbook' understanding of wet-rice cultivation technique with an appreciation that there are often good reasons for not applying supposedly 'advanced' methods (and that farmers' ignorance is rarely one of those reasons!). For example, while he applauds a general tendency in northern Sierra Leone to switch from broadcasting to transplanting because less seed is required, the field is more uniform, yields are higher and there is less weed (because the swamp is weeded before it is transplanted), he is shrewd enough to appreciate that it must remain 'the practice to establish the crop early by broadcasting' in swamps subject to sudden flood or rapid flow of water at transplanting time. He is also sensitive to the significance of a number of local adaptations which greatly improve the appeal of swamp cultivation, e.g. dry-season cultivation of sweet potatoes, cassava, tobacco and vegetables. These dry-season crops were doing 'much to popularize swamp cultivation, as well as relieving the pressure on uplands to some extent'.

Glanville then makes two crucial observations: that 'the utilization of inland swamps has been a natural growth...swamp cultivation was begun by local farmers without outside assistance' and that the principal contribution of Government had been to support these changes with propaganda and practical assistance. One important example of this kind of practical assistance had been to establish a 'revolving scheme' for supplying Scarcies farmers with seeds of new rice varieties. The Agricultural Officer in charge of this scheme (Roddan?) concluded that the success of the scheme (evident in 'the daily queue of farmers...waiting just to give in their names to receive assistance from the Seed Distribution Scheme') clearly demonstrated 'that the way to gain the confidence of the farmer is to assist him in growing his own crops' (Department of Agriculture

Annual Report for 1936, p. 11). Encouraged by this success, a number of other 'populist' initiatives were attempted, or came to fruition, under Glanville's directorship of the Department of Agriculture, 1944–51.

Populism as a policy perspective

In 1938 the Leverhulme Trust invited four members of Parliament to visit West Africa:

To investigate, study and report on the West African colonies generally; the inter-relationship between the Government, its officials, the traders and the natives; the status and standard of life of the native population and improvement thereof; the production of food and other materials and the increase thereof; and, in particular, certain main problems in respect of the development of agricultural, pastoral and forestry resources.

A team of four technical experts was appointed to accompany the party. Subsequently, the West Africa Commission (as it was known) issued two technical reports, one concerning crop production and soil fertility and the other concerning livestock. The report on agriculture (Sampson & Crowther, 1943) summarizes the case for greater concentration on food crops and endorses the policy initiatives undertaken in Nigeria by Faulkner.

The lessons of the Indian experience had earlier been advocated to the other agriculture departments in British West Africa following the appointment of Sir Frank Stockdale as the first agricultural adviser to the Colonial Secretary in 1929. Stockdale, former Director of the Ceylon Department of Agriculture, a department with a considerable record of achievement in food-crop research (Pain, 1983), toured West Africa in 1929, and on his recommendation R.R. Glanville visited Madras and Ceylon to study South Asian techniques of wet-rice cultivation (Glanville, 1933). One of the authors of the West Africa Commission report on crops and soils had accompanied Stockdale on that earlier mission. The wisdom of this earlier advice had been confirmed by the world trade recession of the 1930s, when prices for many African export crops fell to a half or a quarter the peak levels they had reached in the 1920s. Food-crop cultivators were often better able to withstand the shock of recession than farmers in districts heavily dependent on export production.

The second major point endorsed by the West Africa Commission is an emerging consensus among some of the more perceptive observers of African agriculture that West African farmers were excellent judges of soils. Local practices, the report argues, contained many hints that researchers might follow up with benefit. Igbo farmers in eastern Nigeria already planted fallows with the quick-growing tree *Acioa barteri* to help speed up the process of soil regeneration, and practiced composting. On the other hand, the report pointedly observes, 'some...agricultural officers seemed to assume that compost could only be made where animal droppings and urine were available' (Sampson & Crowther, 1943: 36).

Where farmers departed from 'textbook' recommendations the possibility is entertained that the textbooks might be wrong (or at least have underestimated the difficulties):

Is it possible that at some earlier time the plough was tried in Nigeria and abandoned? Does the marked wash of soil from the ridges of ploughed land into the furrow indicate that the soil crumbs are not sufficiently stable to stand up indefinitely to ploughing...? (p. 54).

The report is not slow to point out that research often tends to confirm the value of local practices:

When green manuring was first introduced it was naturally assumed that its main benefit would come from the atmospheric nitrogen fixed by the bacteria in the nodules of the leguminous plants. Field experiments showed, however, that spreading the ashes left after burning a cut and wilted green manure crop gave just as good results on the following food crops as burying the whole of the crop. Removing the ashes from the plots caused a marked loss of fertility. Mineral elements mobilised by the green manure crops are thus more important than the atmospheric nitrogen fixed by it. Soil analyses showed that the ashes increased the supply of exchangeable bases in the soil (p. 37).

In short, science had discovered the value of 'bush burning'. If this was the first, it was certainly to be far from the last occasion on which researchers in West Africa were to 'reinvent' traditional agriculture! Even at the time of the West Africa Commission's visit, the Nigerian Department of Agriculture, having experienced difficulties with Allen cotton not unlike those earlier described for Sierra Leone, was trying 'to resuscitate the old-established cottons of this part of Africa', these having survived 'in a few out-of-the-way places...in spite of [earlier] prohibitions...' (pp. 38–9).

The Commission draws some obvious lessons from this kind of experience. More could and should be done with local crop varieties and cultivation techniques. They draw attention in particular to local legumes ('we cannot help thinking that more should be done with existing leguminous crops') and to intercropping ('the circumstance that inter-cropping is almost universal throughout tropical Africa is in itself strong presumptive evidence of some direct benefit').

Howard Jones, one-time mycologist in the Nigerian Department of Agriculture, had already reflected upon the latter point in a book on West African agriculture published in 1936.

The plants are not growing at random, but have been planted at proper distances on hillocks of soil arranged in such a way that when rain falls it does not waterlog the plants, nor does it pour off the surface and wash away the fine soil: the stumps of bushes and trees are left for the yams to climb upon and the oil palms are left standing because they yield valuable fruits: and although several kinds of plants are growing together, they were not sown at the same time nor will they be reaped together: they are rather successive crops planted in such a way that the soil is always occupied and is neither dried up by the sun nor leached out by the rain, as it would be if it were left bare at any time (Jones, 1936: pp. 34–5).

A populist programme would be a logical next step from insights of this kind. 'It is possible', Sampson & Crowther (1943: 34) suggest, in an especially succinct summary of the populist argument 'that the systematic study of mixed cropping and other native practices might lead to comparatively minor modifications in Yoruba and other forms of agriculture, which might in the aggregate do more to increase crop production and soil fertility than revolutionary changes to green manuring or mixed farming'.

Such an approach, however, implied long-term, patient research, with a particular emphasis on 'base line' surveys of the kind undertaken by Glanville in the Scarcies, or by agricultural officers in northern Ghana (cf. Lynn, 1942). To this end the West Africa Commission advocated less parsimonious research funding, and the creation of new 'field survey' units.

We have in mind something much more far-reaching than the mere co-ordinating and filing of an indigestible mass of facts. We regard the central purpose [of survey activities of this sort] as the ecological interpretation of the country and its mode of life (p.53).

The great advantage of this new 'ecological' emphasis would be that it employed the same kinds of land-use categories and concepts employed by local farmers, it would make use of 'local traditions' and it would be possible 'to employ African assistants to do work for which they are already well qualified, whatever their standard of book learning' (Sampson & Crowther, 1943: 53).

Populism versus 'high technology' initiatives

The alternative to a strategy based on support for indigenous farming practices was a technologically-intensive approach by-passing the peasantry. Wartime conditions in Sierra Leone provided an opportunity for the merits of these rival approaches to be put to the test.

Freetown, with its huge natural harbour, was a major strategic base for the Allied war effort. The wartime population of Freetown created major new food supply demands. Perhaps in something of a panic, policy makers opted for a 'high tech' irrigation approach. An Irrigation and Drainage Branch was established in 1941–2, and with a 'grant cum loan' from the Colonial Welfare and Development Fund of £303,000, embarked on the construction of large-scale rice polders in the Scarcies and elsewhere.

The results were not encouraging, however. The Annual Reports of the Department of Agriculture from 1942 to 1946 mention teething problems and staffing difficulties. The extent of these difficulties may be judged from the fact that when the war ended an irrigation consultant was brought in to advise on the future of the scheme. He thought the scheme unworkable. Small-scale experiments continued, however, because as the Annual Report for 1948 rightly noted, 'the problems associated with irrigation agriculture...are complex and much fundamental work is desirable.' In consequence, the polder at Rokupr was monitored carefully for a number of seasons. Yields began to decline from the outset (Figure 1) and soils were found to suffer from increased acidity and toxic concentrations of iron and aluminium salts. By 1948 average yields on the monitored plots had declined to 31 per cent of their level in 1944 when the polder was constructed. The solution was to reinstate local cultivation practices. The 1949 Report records that 'the success of reverting to the utilization of natural and unrestricted irrigation by tidal river water [was] astonishing' (cf. Fig. 1).

R.R. Glanville had been appointed Director of Agriculture in 1944, and when the immediate pressures of wartime lifted the Department of Agriculture took up once more the threads of the pre-war approach towards agricultural development. The 1947

32

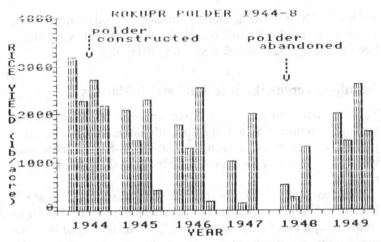

Figure 1 Rice yields on four poldered plots, Rokupr, 1944-9

Annual Report re-states the case for a policy based on careful trials and work with peasant farmers, and stresses the continued dynamism of farmer initiatives in rice cultivation, pointing to the success of Temne migrants to the Rotifunk area in opening up mangrove swamp cultivation in the Bumpeh Creek, with the consequent adoption of this technique by local farmers in Moyamba District.

Two populist initiatives from this period deserve special notice. A vocabulary of plant names in Sierra Leonian languages, compiled over many years by F.C. Deighton, the Njala plant pathologist, was reported to be complete in manuscript form. Though not published until eight years later (Deighton, 1957) this has since proved to be invaluable to fieldworkers interested in Sierra Leonian farming systems and agricultural botany. The second initiative concerns work on indigenous principles of land use undertaken by the Njala soil chemist. H.W. Dougall's work on bush burning has already been mentioned. His work on a catenary land-use system at Rosino, one of the polder sites, was perhaps of even greater significance:

A land-use system in the seep zone (which extends from the bottom of the lower footslopes to the margin of the rear area) has been evolved by the local Africans themselves. It is on this pale, brownish-grey and reddish-brown colluvium that they establish their rice nurseries, cassava and sweet potato beds and occasional small banana groves. It is doubtful if the system could be profitably improved upon... (Department of Agriculture Annual Report for 1949, pp.26–7).

His work pinpointed a crucial weakness of the original polder scheme, namely that it:

envisaged only reclaiming for the cultivation of rice, the hydrophilous marsh grassland behind the river's flood plain. It did not take cognizance of Rosino as a 'unit of landscape' of which the marsh grassland formed an integral part.

Dougall's appreciation of the need for detailed study 'of the complete landscape form' to arrive at appropriate land-use proposals was a most important insight. Much of the skill in indigenous farming practices in Sierra Leone (and indeed in African peasant agriculture more generally) lies in the integration of valley and upland land use. Lack of attention to this point continues to bedevil a number of agricultural planning initiatives today.

The 1949 Annual Report announced 'the constitution of the long-mooted Soil Conservation and Land Utilization team'. The substantial report (Waldock, Capstick & Browning, 1951) was published two years later. It is in effect an answer to the call by the West Africa Commission for work directed towards better understanding of indigenous land-use practices, and matches in theme and treatment a number of similar ecological studies undertaken more or less contemporaneously in other British African territories (cf. Allen, 1949; 1965; Trapnell, 1943; Grove, 1951).

It might be supposed, therefore, that agricultural policy in Sierra Leone was now well-set for the future, with detailed ecological research as the foundation for a peasant-focused development strategy on populist lines. This was not to be. The 1949 Annual Report, while celebrating the return of gradualist, populist, policies also sounded a significant new note. The first page of the Report acknowledges a new impetus from Mr Childs' *Plan for Economic Development for Sierra Leone* (published 1949), 'which includes a five-year programme to increase agricultural production' in which 'the general emphasis has been on increased production, with the introduction of mechanical aids to save labour and increase output...'.

Dougall resigned in 1950, and his successor was not appointed until more than a year had elapsed. The relevant files having disappeared in the interval, the new soil chemist reported that he was unable to continue Dougall's experiments. Glanville retired in 1951, and the new director, G.W. Lines, devoted his energies to promoting the Mechanical Cultivation Scheme called for in the Childs Plan. According to the Annual Report for 1951: 'this mechanized production of swamp rice, together with experimentation and extension with fertilizers...will form the basis of policy for the department for the immediate future and, it is hoped, for many years to come' (p.1).

The rapid eclipse of the populist tendency in Sierra Leone, and the return to favour of technology-intensive approaches to agricultural development, notwithstanding the sobering lessons of the wartime experience, were part of a general trend in British West Africa, in which the pressures of post-war commodity shortages and new ideas promoted by the Labour government in Westminster, 1945–51, fundamentally reshaped colonial development policies (Pearce, 1982). As Britain 'emerged from the war impoverished, with a growing population, new social priorities and a new science of human nutrition' (Beresford, 1975: 11) British agriculture, badly depressed in the 1920s and 1930s, underwent a major revival. The techniques and outlook associated with this revival appear to have exerted a strong influence over post-war colonial agricultural development initiatives.

A number of the projects spawned at this time (most notoriously, the Tanganyika groundnut scheme) have since come to serve as object lessons in how not to undertake agricultural development. By the standards of the Niger Agricultural Project at Mokwa (in central Nigeria) where the equipment was inappropriate for local soil conditions and exceptionally difficult to service, and where tractors cultivated larger areas than farmers had labour to weed (Baldwin, 1957), or the high farce of another Nigerian project (a rice scheme in the Benue valley) where newly imported crawler tractors were unable to work during the first year because the garage built for them during the dry season turned out to be located on an island in the wet, tractorization in Sierra Leone went relatively smoothly. Rice could be grown successfully in the infertile and difficult to cultivate boliland swamps, and in riverine grasslands around Torma Bum, where previously labour shortages had restricted output. Local communities adapted their farming methods and social arrangements to accommodate mechanization, and were keen for the scheme to be expanded (Jedrej, 1983).

The main problems with tractor mechanization in Sierra Leone were economic (Gleave, 1977). Even during a period of relative prosperity (due to the rapid expansion of diamond mining) in the

1950s it proved difficult to finance the scheme on a self-supporting basis. More recently, as the terms of trade for Sierra Leonian exports deteriorated and foreign exchange shortages intensified, tractor ploughing has required increasingly heavy subsidies. In the late 1970s rates charged to farmers for tractor hiring were only about 40 per cent of the full cost per hectare. Starkey (1981) notes that 90 per cent of the cost of tractor ploughing has ultimately to be paid for in foreign exchange.

Perhaps the most problematic aspect of the Mechanical Cultivation Scheme in Sierra Leone was that at its greatest extent in the late 1950s only about 4 per cent of the country's total rice output was produced by tractor cultivation, but the scheme accounted for 80 per cent of the Department of Agriculture's expenditure. In 1956 a total of 15,000 acres was ploughed by tractor, but the Annual Report for 1957 estimates that a further 75,000 acres would need to be added if rice grown under the scheme was to be sufficient to replace the 36,700 tons of rice imported in 1956.

During the later 1950s and then during the 1960s there was some case for pressing on with tractor mechanization because of the short-term dislocations in the agricultural economy caused by the boom in diamond mining from c. 1955 onwards. Many younger farmers and farm labourers left their villages to try their hand at diamond mining, and the rice harvest suffered accordingly. The flow of labour from farming to mining began to dry up during the 1970s and may now be in reverse. The rice import bill is still high, but the current view is that subsidized mechanization can only be a small part of the overall agricultural development strategy because it ties up resources badly needed for a more broadly-based agricultural development programme.

The same point has been made for other West African countries. Hart (1982) enthuses over the recent 'success' of mechanized rice production in northern Ghana, but Shepherd (1981) paints a very different picture in which tractorized production is dependent on both overt and hidden subsidies from the state. Goody (1980: footnotes) cites an unpublished report by Ackroyd detailing the extent to which this mechanized rice production initiative was 'non-economic'. In addition to subsidies on fertilizer (85 per cent in 1976), land clearance costs and machinery hire, participants in the scheme benefited from restrictions on rice imports, import concessions for farm machinery, and an 'overvalued' currency which made imported machinery and fuel relatively cheap in real terms.

Whatever the arguments for using state revenues to boost the initial stages of an agricultural revolution, schemes based on subsidies on this scale must be called into question by the severity of the current economic crisis in West Africa. It is in the face of dilemmas of this sort that the 'still, small voice' of populism is beginning once again to attract an audience. In 1981, Sierra Leone imported 55,114 tons of rice. Many would argue that it is a priority to replace such imports with home-grown rice. The comparative advantage calculations are in the country's favour (Pearson, Stryker & Humphreys, 1981). The question is whether to do this by further mechanization, or by a programme of 'mass mobilization' of the peasantry. Looked at from the mechanization point of view the target is 55,000 tons of rice. From the populist point of view the target may be put in another way: an additional output of 5 bushels of clean rice per household.

Postscript – lessons for today?

Since Independence there have been three main phases in debates about agricultural policy in West Africa: a phase in the first decade after Independence in which it was argued that the agricultural sector should be 'milked' to provide resources for industrial take-off, a phase, beginning about 1970, of renewed emphasis on agricultural investment and on small-holder agriculture in particular, and (most recently) signs of a renewed interest in populist perspectives. I shall conclude this chapter with brief comments on each of these issues.

Agriculture and import-substitution industrialization

Despite the fact that the majority of export earnings came from the agricultural sector, planning scenarios in the decade after Independence rarely gave farmers the attention they deserved. In Nigeria, for example, projected agricultural expenditure under the first two economic plans after Independence (1962–6 and 1970–4) was 13.5 per cent and 13.8 per cent of total planned public-sector investment; this in a country in which, at the time, agriculture accounted for approximately 50 per cent of GDP. The pattern was repeated through much of the rest of West Africa, with Ivory Coast a major exception.

This neglect was quite deliberate. Since peasant farmers had continued 'to deliver the goods' under a degree of colonial benign neglect, they might be left to continue. The main route to modernization was thought to be through industrialization. Accordingly, as much as possible development capital was reserved for the urban/industrial sector. The main strategy was 'import substitution industrialization': concentration on manufactured goods prominent on the import list. Typically, those that were easiest to tackle were consumer goods, many of them relative luxuries, such as beer and cigarettes.

In some cases revenues for import substitution were derived from surpluses accumulated by export produce marketing boards. Marketing boards were first introduced in the early days of the Second World War, ostensibly to keep order in a shrinking market. After the war ended the marketing board arrangement was continued and extended to cover other export crops. The idea was that marketing boards would hold back a portion of the world market price in good years in order to subsidize producer prices in bad years. This, it was thought, would encourage orderly expansion of export crop agriculture, as well as acting as a deflationary device to control the level of imports. During the period of post-war economic expansion prices for African exports rose rapidly. By the middle 1950s export earnings were, in real terms, three to four times greater than in the 1930s. The majority of years between 1945 and 1960 proved to be good ones for commodities such as cocoa and groundnuts. During these years the marketing boards accumulated large reserves later drawn upon to support the import-substitution industrialization strategy (Forrest, 1981).

The problem with input-substitution strategies was that they failed, in the short-term at least, to stimulate an industrial revolution. The legacy of this failure, so a number of authorities now argue, is a high level of poverty and unemployment in urban areas, while the agricultural sector has been dangerously weakened by lack of investment and by tax pressures (Bates, 1981; Forrest, 1981; Williams, 1981).

Integrated agricultural development

From the early 1970s onwards policy makers began to accept that much more attention would need to be paid to the agricultural sector. Because large-scale mechanized agriculture had a poor record in most countries, and the bulk of both agricultural exports and food supplies still derived from the peasant sector, much of this attention began, quite rightly, to be paid to small-scale producers. Equity was an additional consideration. Without the immediate prospect of an urban-based industrial revolution it would be important to try and reduce rates of urban migration, and to improve the attractiveness of economic opportunities in rural areas.

International aid programmes moved to support this new emphasis on rural development (World Bank, 1975). Small-farmer projects became a dominant emphasis in World Bank lending policies for African countries. Many of these projects were granted low-interest funding from the International Development Association, an affiliate of the World Bank set up to assist long-term development objectives in the poorest countries. As in the 1930s, food production issues assumed some prominence among policy makers and planners.

The emphasis in most of these small-farmer projects is on what is sometimes termed a 'biological package' of fertilizer and 'improved' high-yielding crop varieties, as distinct from a 'technological' package based, for example, on mechanized cultivation or pump irrigation. Typically, technological packages benefit only the larger-scale farmers able to afford the expense of the initial inputs. The idea behind the biological package approach is that the benefits will be accessible to a broader range of farmers.

High-yielding varieties and other components of the biological package are the results of research carried out by a network of international research stations, including the International Institute of Tropical Agriculture (IITA) at Ibadan Nigeria, co-ordinated by the Consultative Group on International Agricultural Research (CGIAR). In many cases, these inputs are supplied to farmers through regional development agencies known as Integrated Agricultural (or Rural) Development Projects (IADPs or IRDPs). Typically, these projects supply small-scale farmers with seed or seedlings, fertilizer, credit to purchase the input package, and extension advice. Generally, they also have some responsibility for solving some of the most urgent infrastructure and social welfare constraints on increased agricultural production in the area concerned. Many IADPs build farm access roads, improve village water supplies and take some interest in health and nutrition matters. Where this is ecologically appropriate, IADPs will tend to maintain a balance in interest between food crops for domestic consumption and 'export' crops. Much of the initial funding for

IADPs in Africa came from the World Bank, but now bilateral aid agencies and the African Development Bank are also heavily involved.

Populism revisited

To what extent has this renewed emphasis on the small farmer succeeded? The evidence from a range of evaluation studies across West Africa (e.g. Adams, 1981; Airey, Binns & Mitchell, 1979; Conti, 1979; Lappia, 1980; Karimu & Richards, 1981; Shepherd, 1981; Williams, 1981) is that so far the results have been disappointing. There is little sign yet of anything equivalent to the Green Revolution in Asia in the 1960s. Few projects seem capable of gaining and sustaining the interest of dedicated farmers, and drop-out rates are often high.

Two main types of explanation have been offered for the apparent failure of IADP development to stimulate a self-sustaining agricultural revolution. The first is couched in terms of political economy. Either IADP development was never intended to benefit small farmers, but simply to ensnare them (through indebtedness to a project) within a web of capitalist (or state-controlled) relations of production (Williams, 1981), or it cannot work as intended because of state interventions in the marketing process. This latter line of argument assumes that governments are especially vulnerable to pressure from urban interests, and respond by 'subsidizing' urban food prices, at the expense of peasant producers. Food aid, and cheap imports paid for in an 'overvalued' currency are two of the ways this is done, so it has been suggested (cf. Levi, 1976; Bates, 1981). A second line of argument reserves judgement on issues of this sort, pointing instead to the inappropriateness of the input packages on offer. Shepherd (1981: 189), commenting on two IADP-type projects in northern Ghana, notes that whereas 'both these projects try to propagate "appropriate" innovations' neither has allowed for 'sufficient research, nor sufficient farmer participation and influence in planning and implementation to be confident of what appropriate innovations might be'. In a similar vein, a recent evaluation of an IADP in central Nigeria (Bivens, 1984) concludes that the small-farmer elements in the programme showed the best rate of return, that other elements were counter-productive, and that much more attention should now be paid to farming techniques already developed by small farmers in the project area. 'The small farmer's mixed cropping system is far more productive than earlier believed. It should be the starting point for future efforts to raise agricultural production...' (Bivens, 1984:4).

A number of commentators on agricultural change in Africa, and the tropics more generally, are now beginning to work through the implications of judgements of this sort. Recent literature has laid special stress on a revived populism as a vital 'missing ingredient' in technology generation. Green (1983) notes that agricultural development programmes are lacking, most crucially, in 'packages of inputs/technique changes which are tested, practicable and economically viable and related to local (often very local) contexts'. Biggs (1984) suggests that failure to generate locally-relevant inputs reflects a situation in which projects insulate themselves from the very contacts they should be fostering – i.e. with farmers themselves. 'Feedback', even in projects committed on paper to 'problem-solving' approaches, is often purely nominal. Some IADPs have no mechanisms through which extension workers could report farmers' views, needs, and reactions, and experts are not accountable for the recommendations they make. Dey (1981: 122), discussing rice development schemes in the Gambia, argues that 'by failing to take into account the complexities of the existing farming system and concentrating on men to the exclusion of women, the irrigated rice projects have lost, in the technical sense that valuable available female expertise was wasted'. Chambers (1983) now more boldly asserts a point tentatively outlined by the West Africa Commission forty years earlier: indigenous agricultural knowledge, despite being ignored or overridden by consultant experts, is 'the single largest knowledge resource not yet mobilized in the development enterprise'. There can be little doubt, therefore, that populism is firmly back on the rural development agenda. In consequence, the lessons of populist interludes in the history of colonial agricultural development in West Africa, as outlined in this chapter, assume a renewed significance.

2 The ecology of West African farming systems:

I Seasonality and shifting cultivation

Introduction

This and the following chapter attempt to summarize some of the ecological principles on which small-holder agriculture in West Africa rests. Agricultural environments in tropical and temperate latitudes differ in a number of important ways. For example, seasonality in the tropics is a function of rainfall, not temperature, and species diversity in the natural vegetation tends (in more forested environments) to be greater than in temperate regions. This makes for very complex ecological relationships – a complexity which the farmer often seeks to emulate, as in intercropping, for example – and great local diversity in agricultural management practices.

The bulk of scientific research on farming has been undertaken in temperate regions, and this knowledge has sometimes proved a poor, or misleading, guide to the problems faced by tropical farmers. It is possible to design a farming system 'package' for the temperate world with some chance that it might be applicable over a wide area. This is often not the case in tropical regions. The significance of this point is redoubled in West Africa, where, because of low population densities, farmers seek to make the best of natural conditions – to capitalize on local diversity – rather than embark on labour-demanding schemes to impose greater uniformity and control on the farming environment. This is one reason why the terracing and irrigation systems found in some parts of Asia have rarely been possible, or necessary, in West Africa. But if the majority of West African farmers have little time (literally) for the creation of a uniform, controlled, farming environment, they more than make up for this 'lack' (if indeed it is a lack) by their skills in the management of natural conditions – their ability to make a living from an understanding of diverse, varied and complex ecological relationships. This ecological knowledge, so I shall argue, is one of the most significant of rural Africa's resources, and development and educational agencies must learn how to tap into it and harness it for 'nation building' purposes.

At present, rural knowledge of ecological processes is an area of skill formation which tends to be treated solely as a 'hang-over' from the past. This is a legacy of a view (still surviving in some quarters) that saw West African farming systems as the lowest rung on an evolutionary ladder. Because West African farmers tended to ride with, rather than override, natural diversity, it was assumed that their techniques were especially 'ancient' and 'primitive'.

Arguments of the 'my goodness, they haven't yet invented irrigation/the wheel/the plough' kind were especially common in the early colonial period. A 'mental map' shared by a number of officials was that rainfall was inversely correlated with quality of farming and level of 'civilization'. Lady Lugard (1906), a journalist, and wife of the first Governor General of Nigeria, thought that 'the uplands bordering upon the desert were the most desirable portions of the Negro belt' and that 'the races which inhabited them were maintained by climatic conditions on a higher platform of mental and moral activity than the more supine inhabitants of the denser tropical regions to the south.' G.C. Dudgeon, agricultural adviser for the British West African territories, wrote that in the Eastern Province of Southern Nigeria 'farming is generally of poor quality until the region of high rainfall is left.' He had a similar view of conditions west of the Niger: 'the Benis often [plant] their grain crops in only partially cleared land. Further to the north in the same province a better system is noticeable among the Ishans, Ifons and people of Agbede'. The Yoruba, in drier country to the west, are especially commended 'for the depth of their cultivation [which] in some measure compensates for the non-employment of manure' (Dudgeon, 1911: 89).

Few modern agronomists would make similar distinctions between Igbo and Bini farming practices on the one hand and Ishan, Ifon and Yoruba practices on the other. The differences of which Dudgeon writes would now be understood as local adaptations to rainfall intensity, soil texture and erosion risks (much greater, for example, in areas around, say, Benin and Owerri, where high rainfall is combined with soils derived from unconsolidated Tertiary sands, than in parts of Oyo and Bendel States where much heavier, more fertile soils derive from granites of the Basement Complex).

As shown in the previous chapter, many colonial agricultural officers had learnt by the 1930s and 1940s to distrust arguments of the sort advanced by Dudgeon. The proper test for any practice was whether it worked in the environment concerned, not whether it looked 'advanced' or 'backward'. Testing requires carefully controlled input–output trails. If 'shallow' cultivation on 'partially-cleared' land gives better returns relative to the inputs expended than rival systems, and if these results can be sustained over time, then the technique is a good one, irrespective of whether it was invented yesterday or a thousand years ago.

The older ideas, however, live on, or reappear in more sophisticated form, in a number of text-books, where they are often the basis for the argument that the key to agricultural development in Africa lies in 'technology transfer' – the importation of 'appropriate' agricultural inputs from tropical regions held to be more 'advanced' on the evolutionary scale.

This line of argument, apparent in Stockdale's insistence on the relevance of experience in South India to agricultural development in colonial West Africa (Ch.1), reappears in, for example, Jack Goody's *Technology, tradition and the state in Africa* (1971: 76), where he concludes that Africa failed to match 'the developments in productivity and skill, stratification and specialization, that marked the agrarian societies of early medieval Europe' because Africa lacked a Feudal, 'intermediate', technology, based on the wheel and plough. This lack Goody judges 'is of critical importance in the developments of the present day'.

By contrast, this book argues that agricultural development programmes should put aside 'evolutionary' assumptions when dealing with unfamiliar agricultural practices, seek out the principles upon which these practices are based, and aim to assist further development of their implications. The material in this and the next chapter is used to demonstrate that this is an approach which has already begun to bear fruit. West African farmers can no longer be castigated for 'wasteful' burning of vegetation, 'merely scratching the surface' of their soils, 'failing' to plough deeper, or lazily mixing their crops together in an arbitrary and unhygienic manner. Practices such as 'minimum tillage' (Lal, 1979a) and 'intercropping' (Steiner, 1982) are now seen not as evidence of the 'backwardness' of African agriculture, but as principles with considerable development potential. They are even beginning to attract the attention of commercial agriculture in temperate lands, thus bringing into focus once again Stamp's idea that the European and North American farmer might learn much from African soil management techniques. This would be ironic revenge indeed on an earlier generation of evolutionary 'Grand Theorists' for their speculations concerning the 'backwardness' of African agriculture.

Seasonality

Nearly the whole of West Africa lies in the tropical zone of seasonal rainfall (as distinct from the equatorial zone of year-round rainfall). Rainfall-dependent seasonality raises a set of problems for the cultivator which differs from those raised by temperature-dependent seasonality, the kind which dominates agricultural operations in temperate latitudes (Harris, 1980).

In southern Europe, North Africa and the Middle East the bulk of rainfall comes in winter, and crops ripen during a dry summer. In the tropical zone not only are rainfall intensities and rates of evaporation high by comparison with temperate latitudes, but also the peak of biological activity in terms of plant growth coincides with the periods of maximum rainfall, and greatest cloud cover. In addition, rainfall is often especially unreliable at the start and end of the rainy season when decisions about planting and harvesting have to be made, and tropical day lengths are short (varying in summer from 12 hours at the equator to c. 14 hours at the tropic) by comparison with summertime day lengths in temperate latitudes (up to a maximum of 20 hours in mid-summer at 60° N). In consequence, tropical-zone crops have to be adapted to considerable degrees of drought stress at the beginning and end of the rainy season, to relatively short periods of daylight, and to fairly cloudy conditions at the height of the growing season (Kowal & Kassam, 1978).

Contrary to popular impression, annual rainfall variability – measured in terms of standard deviations from mean annual totals – is often no greater in magnitude in West Africa than it is in temperate latitudes. From the farmer's point of view, however, annual data are not very meaningful. The key issues for West African cultivators are the dates of the beginning and end of the rainy season, and the variability of rainfall at those times (Jackson, 1977). Variability of rainfall in the opening and closing months of the rainy season is commonly as high as 40–60 per cent of the long-term average for the months in question. This problem can be severe in forested high-rainfall districts as well as in drier savanna regions. High variability is also associated with the mid-season 'break' (the 'little dry-season') in areas of double-maximum rainfall distribution. It is a moot point, therefore, whether rainfall variability in the case illustrated in Figure 2 – Okitipupa, a coastal area on the western edge of the Niger Delta, with high annual rainfall totals (an average of 2100 mm for the period 1937–63), but with a double-maximum distribution and high rural population densities

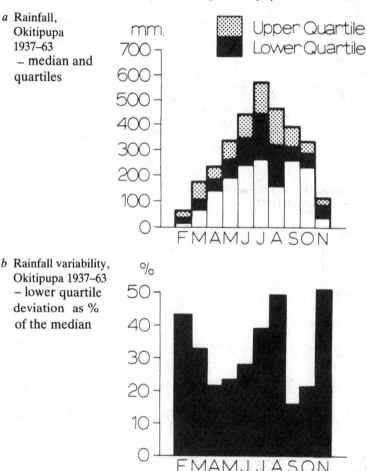

a Rainfall, Okitipupa 1937–63 – median and quartiles

b Rainfall variability, Okitipupa 1937–63 – lower quartile deviation as % of the median

Figure 2   Rainfall variability in a high rainfall area

(over 100 persons/km^2) – might not in fact be a problem of greater agricultural significance than rainfall variability in the lightly populated Sahel. Apart from the extreme south-eastern corner of Nigeria, even the wettest districts in West Africa have a strongly-marked dry season. Figure 3 shows soil moisture balances for

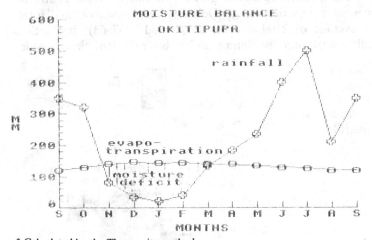

* Calculated by the Thornwaite method
Source: Richards (1977).

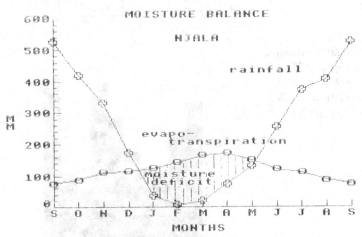

+ Calculated according to the Papadakis formula
Source: van Vuure *et al.* (1972).

Figure 3 Dry season moisture deficits at two high-rainfall stations

Okitipupa, and for Njala, a high-rainfall station in the western sector of the West African forest zone with an annual average rainfall of 2750 mm. Both stations suffer a severe negative moisture balance in the dry season: evapotranspiration runs in excess of rainfall from early November until mid-March in Okitipupa and from mid-December until the last week of April in Njala.

Throughout West Africa farmers are acutely sensitive to the problem of drought at the start of the cultivation cycle. Ways of coping with these uncertainties vary from area to area. Most communities have developed a range of forecasting techniques. Shifts in wind patterns and cloud formations are closely observed and plant, insect and bird activity monitored to assess changes in soil and atmospheric moisture levels. In parts of southern Nigeria, farmers assess the approach of the rainy season by noting the timing of fresh, red leaves on the tree known in Yoruba as **eki** (*Lophira alata*). In central Sierra Leone the flowering of **gbota** (*Antrocaryon micraster*[?]) conveys the same message. Farmers from Igboho in the savannas of western Nigeria rely on the following signs that rain is near and planting should begin (Oguntoyinbo & Richards, 1978):

1 Leafing of **iroko** (*Chlorophora excelsa*) and baobab *(Adansonia digitata)*
2 Sky signs, e.g. 'first the sky shows red and after a few days or weeks clouds will begin to form'.
3 Shifts in wind direction and cloud formations, e.g. 'rising heat', (i.e. convection), distant thunder.
4 Bird song indicators, e.g. the call of the dove **konkoto** (*Streptopelia semitorquata* [?]) ceases.

Although these forecasting techniques, and their efficacy, have been little studied by climatologists, they are especially significant where (as is often the case) crucial decisions relating to cultivation have to be taken in advance of the rains, or in the interval between the first few storms and steady rain. Leaf indicators may be especially useful, since many West African trees are triggered into new growth by the transition from dry continental to moist oceanic atmospheric conditions preceding the rains (Lely, 1925).

In many parts of the forest zone where rotational fallowing is still practised, the timing of bush burning is an issue of vital significance. A good burn increases soil fertility and inhibits weeds and insect activity. A poor burn leaves farmers stretched for labour, since unburnt vegetation must be chopped up and piled into bonfires for piecemeal burning. To obtain a good burn, the farmer needs to leave vegetation to dry for as long as possible. Sappy vegetation over moisture-retentive soils, for example, may not be dry enough underneath for the fire to gain a real hold unless the brush wood is left for several weeks to dry out thoroughly. But this then courts the risk that the farm will be caught by any unseasonally early heavy rainstorms, leaving the farm owner in a worse position than if the burn had been attempted too soon. Not surprisingly, then, the issue of precisely when to burn elicits a great deal of theorization, experimentation and argument. Farmers are acutely conscious of the moisture-retentive properties of different soils, and how this might affect the burn, and of the combustible properties of different types of vegetation (in Sierra Leone, farmers greatly value *Dialium guinense* in fallow regrowth, because it burns especially fiercely). For farmers using bush-fallowing methods, unseasonally early rainfall (because of the way in which it disturbs the burn) is as great a hazard as drought. In central Sierra Leone there have been at least 12 years, from 1912 to date, in which heavy rainfall in February and March severely disrupted bush burning, with major consequences for the rice harvest (it has been estimated that in some years this factor alone has reduced yields on upland rice farms by up to 20–30 per cent: Scotland, 1919; Richards, 1985).

More usually, however, it is late rainfall which causes problems. Farmers cope with this hazard in a variety of ways, e.g. by staggered planting, by planting special early-season drought resistant varieties of crops, by mulching crops to conserve moisture, or by treating planting materials in such a way that they remain dormant in the soil until soil moisture passes critical threshold levels. Techniques for inhibiting germination in seed yam, for example, allow planting to take place during the dry season in the Guinea Savanna in Nigeria (Atteh, 1980; Diehl, 1981). One of the most important and widespread techniques for spreading the risks associated with early rainfall is the practice of integrating rain-fed cultivation with the cultivation of naturally-flooded valley bottom lands and run-off plots on the lower portions of valley slopes. (This important topic is the subject of detailed examination in Chapters 3 and 4.)

Although early-season rainfall variability poses perhaps the greatest challenge to the managerial inventiveness of the West African farmer, there are other not insignificant aspects of seasonality to be taken into account. West Africa is surprisingly short of

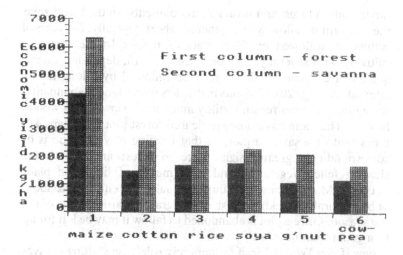

Figure 4 Crop yields in forest and savanna zones compared
Source: Kassam & Kowal (1973).

sunshine during the rainy season. This is especially true of the forest zone where during the height of the rainy season cloud cover can be continuous for days on end, a problem compounded by the short day length characteristic of low latitudes. Figure 4 shows that other things being equal, the sunnier savannas are better suited to the cultivation of most grain and vegetable crops (Kassam & Kowal, 1973). But in order to realize this comparative advantage it would be necessary to make extensive use of irrigation and fertilization. When used according to bush-fallowing methods savanna soils tend to be less fertile and yields less good than on forest soils.

Shifting cultivation

A majority of small-scale farmers in West Africa practice some form of 'shifting cultivation' (or, as some would prefer to call it, since the farms move in a more or less regular sequence about a fixed settlement, 'land rotation fallowing'). Shifting cultivation involves clearing and burning natural vegetation, cultivating the cleared area for a season or two, then moving to a new plot while the old one regains its fertility under natural vegetation regrowth.

There are important differences in the way shifting cultivation is carried out in forest and savanna environments. In the forest zone the cultivation–fallow cycle is generally short: typically, 1–4 years of cultivation followed by 5–15 years of fallow. In the savanna, cultivation for several years – between 2 and 10, depending on the quality of the soil – will generally be followed by a long fallow interval (perhaps 20 or 30 years in districts where land is abundant), since grassy fallows regain fertility much more slowly than woody fallows. The biomass of a newly cleared forest plot is perhaps 4–5 times that of a savanna plot, so that burning of vegetation is of correspondingly greater significance in forest areas, both for clearing felled vegetation and as a means of liberating plant nutrients. Many savannas are burnt annually, but either by accident or by pastoralists seeking a flush of new grass towards the end of the dry season. Once a plot is abandoned to fallow it may be left for up to a generation or more.

Few if any West African farmers rely solely on shifting cultivation. Most commonly, a shifting cultivated 'upland' is combined with some element of valley-bottom 'wet-land' cultivation, or a shifting cultivated 'outfield' is combined with a permanently cultivated, manured and composted 'infield' plot. In some areas, e.g. around some of the larger cities in the savanna, or in densely populated tree-crop farming districts, the shifting cultivation element is of minor proportions or has disappeared entirely (Hill, 1977; Lagemann, 1977; Mortimore, 1971; Ruthenberg, 1980). Nevertheless, I shall argue that the ecological knowledge associated with shifting cultivation continues to provide an important part of the conceptual framework within which West African farmers approach their problems, and for this reason must be understood by agencies contemplating 'populist' strategies of agrarian change.

Two viewpoints have dominated the literature on shifting cultivation: the 'systems' approach and the 'stage' approach.

The systems approach

This approach assumes that shifting cultivation is an integrated set of practices constituting a distinct type of farming enterprise, i.e. a 'farming system'.

Early attitudes to shifting cultivation as a system were almost entirely negative. It was a bad system: exploitative, untidy and misguided. The Parliamentary Under-Secretary of State for the Colonies, W.G.A. Ormsby-Gore, summed up the attitude of the day when noting that in Sierra Leone, for example, 'the natural forest has been ruthlessly destroyed to find virgin soil for the cultivation of "hill" or "land" rice.' (Ormsby-Gore, 1926: 83).

The following passage is characteristic of more recent viewpoints:

A greater understanding of the problems involved, of the advantages of shifting cultivation, and of the difficulties of introducing satisfactory alternative systems has now led to more cautious and balanced assessments both of its merits and of the dangers of trying to change too much too quickly (Ahn, 1970: 233).

This more balanced assessment has been arrived at primarily by considering the ecological relationships involved in 'shifting cultivation' as a system (cf. Nye & Greenland, 1960). This is sometimes referred to as the 'ecosystem' approach (Hopkins, 1974). The ecosystem approach is based on the idea of mapping out the interactions between soils, plants, atmospheric variables and human labour. Key operations include attempts to measure energy inputs (e.g. solar radiation and human labour), to trace 'nutrient flows' within the system, and to measure 'output' (assessed as 'biomass', i.e. total output of organic material, or as 'useful product' harvested).

Earlier attempts to 'model' shifting cultivation in ecosystem terms concentrated on biological variables. More recently, attempts have been made to incorporate economic and social variables into ecosystem models and to link biological and social variables by analysing labour in physiological and nutritional terms (Ruthenberg, 1980; Ellen, 1982). Ideas deriving from the ecosystem approach to African agriculture are discussed in detail in later sections (e.g. in the section on intercropping below).

The stage approach
The stage approach invokes the notion that shifting cultivation belongs to an early rung on the ladder of agricultural progress. This viewpoint owes much to an influential book by Ester Boserup (1965), *The conditions of agricultural growth.*

Her argument has two parts. The first part is based on the notion of 'diminishing returns' to increased investment (in this case diminishing returns to the investment of additional labour on a fixed area of land). She points out that 'permanent' systems of cultivation – e.g. irrigated swamp rice cultivation in South-East Asia – are generally more labour-intensive than shifting cultivation. Extra yield from the more intensive system requires disproportionate extra effort. If land is still in plentiful supply, cultivators are better rewarded by expending their limited energies on extending the area cultivated by shifting cultivation methods than on changing to a more intensive system of cultivation. Permanent cultivation makes more sense where land is in short supply as a result of population growth.

By itself, this part of the argument has no inherent 'evolutionary' implications, but Boserup (1965; 1981), and a number of other writers, e.g. Grigg (1974; 1982) and Wilkinson (1973), go on to treat 'diminishing returns' as the 'driving force' behind agricultural change. Boserup (1965: 17) is quite explicit that her argument about intensity of land use is 'more than just an attempt to identify and classify various types of agriculture existing today and in the past. It is supposed, at the same time, broadly to describe the main stages of the actual evolution of primitive agriculture, during prehistoric times and in the more recent past'.

Accordingly, the second part of the Boserup argument runs as follows. The earliest farming communities inhabited an under-populated world. Enjoying abundant land, but pressed for labour, they would prefer farming systems based on shifting cultivation, since these maximize returns to scarce labour. As population densities began to build up, many farming communities would start to experience land shortages. This would require them to invent (or import) ways of exploiting their land more intensively. At this point 'bush-fallow' methods of restoring soil fertility would be replaced by more labour-intensive methods, e.g. manuring, composting, and crop rotation. Thus, population pressure is seen as a key stimulus to agricultural change. Without it, agricultural communities lack the incentive to develop more elaborate and advanced methods of cultivation.

According to this interpretation, shifting cultivation still 'survives' in West Africa because the region has a long history of under-population. Inikori (1982), for example, advances the argument that the depopulation caused by the slave trade removed one of the key incentives to an African agricultural revolution parallel to the revolution in European agriculture in the eighteenth century. It should be pointed out, however, that Boserup's account is an interesting 'model' rather than history based on detailed evidence. Boserup herself warns us that this is so, though expressing great confidence that the model will turn out to be right in the long run:

...we cannot be sure that systems of extensive land use have preceded the intensive ones in every part of the world, [but] there seems to be little reason to doubt that the typical sequence of development of agriculture has been a gradual change...from extensive to intensive types of land use (Boserup, 1965: 17-18).

Models of this kind are a useful stimulus to historians, archaeologists and others interested in agricultural change in the long run, but I shall want to argue below that they may be quite misleading as a basis for the formulation of agricultural development policies.

Shifting cultivation in West Africa: tradition or innovation?
The Boserup model of agricultural change has to contend with an especially awkward problem. If labour-intensive innovations are unattractive in themselves, and only come about through 'population pressure', can it be said that they represent 'progress'? Some authors, while agreeing that agricultural change takes place as a result of the 'stimulus' of population pressure, argue that these changes are 'involutionary', i.e. they amount to running harder to stay in the same place (cf. Geertz, 1963; Lagemann, 1977), rather than representing a breakthrough to higher levels of agricultural organization.

One of the advantages of the 'systems' approach over the 'stage' approach to shifting cultivation is that it takes no sides in this debate. The systems approach avoids altogether the difficult concept of what constitutes 'progress'. Shifting cultivation and permanent cultivation are different, but one is not necessarily better or more advanced than the other. The only question admitted as relevant by the systems approach is how well does any specific agro-ecosystem work in given environmental and economic circumstances.

This allows for the development of a rather different line of argument. Is it necessary to think of 'permanent cultivation' as a major historical breakthrough? Perhaps West African farming communities have had a knowledge of both types of cultivation from ancient times? This would be no more surprising than the discovery that many groups of so-called hunter-gatherers know how to plant crops, but choose not to utilize this knowledge (Harris, 1980). The significance of this argument is that if knowledge of both shifting and permanent land management systems has been widespread from ancient times, then the extent to which West African farmers use shifting cultivation at any point in time has to be related to specific social and economic conditions.

In a number of other areas of the world – parts of South-East Asia and the Amazon Basin, for example – shifting cultivation is especially associated with the 'pioneer fringe' of new agricultural settlement in lightly-populated districts. Agricultural innovation in such areas is as often a response to new economic incentives as it is to 'population pressure'. Grigg (1974) notes that in the Philippines, for example, the needs of an expanded market for rice in the early part of the twentieth century were met in part from an increase in output of 'hill rice' under shifting cultivation, and not necessarily from the 'more advanced' swamp cultivation system.

Could shifting cultivation in West Africa be interpreted according to this 'pioneer fringe' argument? Certainly the devastation and dislocation caused by the slave trade appears to have encouraged the wilderness, during the nineteenth century, to sweep back over many previously long-settled districts (Ford, 1971). Subsequent recovery might then have called for the application of techniques of 'pioneer' settlement on a large scale. Furthermore, shifting cultivation may, in some areas, have been a good way of responding rapidly to new demands for foodstuffs created by colonial conditions. On this reckoning, then, the extent of shifting cultivation in the early colonial period, rather than signalling the intrinsic 'backwardness' of African agriculture, might be better interpreted as evidence of its innovativeness and responsiveness to changing economic circumstances.

Shifting cultivation: stage, system, or compendium of skills?

Whereas it is a clear advantage of the 'systems' approach that it encourages potentially productive speculations along these lines, there are, nevertheless, some problems associated with the notion that shifting cultivation is a specific farming 'type'. The danger here is of treating the large range of distinct management practices and skills exemplified by the practice of shifting cultivation as if they were part of a single all-or-nothing package. It is on account of this 'package' concept that much of the agricultural development literature in West Africa has been concerned with the question 'how, and with what, shall we replace shifting cultivation?', almost as if shifting cultivation was an enterprise in the same sense as a plantation or cattle ranch.

I want to press an alternative approach, namely a view of shifting cultivation as a rich 'tool kit' of land management procedures in which the value of different items in the 'kit' varies according to nature of the job in hand. The importance of this 'tool kit' view of shifting cultivation is that it allows for the possibility that individual skills and specific elements derived from shifting cultivation may still be of importance even if the overall farming strategy needs to be changed. This is what happens in practice when the West African farmer draws on 'upland' and 'wet-land' or 'infield' and 'outfield' farming methods in the same enterprise. It is a crucial part of my argument, developed at length in later chapters, that the all-or-nothing 'package' view of shifting cultivation – as much a feature of the 'systems' approach as of the 'stage' approach to shifting cultivation – has been a major factor in rendering planners and development agencies blind or insensitive to interesting combinations of this sort.

The following account of shifting cultivation as a compendium of skills is based on the argument that the most effective approach to agricultural change might be to recombine skills and methods already within the shifting cultivator's repertoire rather than design new 'systems' from scratch. Viewed from such a perspective, the experience of shifting cultivation is a major educational resource, in which farmers see at first hand and experiment with a much larger range of soil and vegetation types than would be the case were they shackled to a small permanently-cultivated holding. The experience of complex cycles of fertility decline and fallow renewal thus acquired has equipped many West African farmers with a subtle sense of ecological dynamics with potential significance for the management of long-term side-effects associated with new agricultural technologies.

Resource management skills in shifting cultivation

The reader seeking a full account of the ecology of shifting cultivation in West Africa should turn to studies such as Nye & Greenland (1960), Hopkins (1974), Ahn (1970), and Kowal & Kassam (1978). My comments in this section concentrate on the management skills farmers demonstrate in the process of shifting cultivation, and the relevance of these skills for agricultural development programmes.

Fertility management
Optimum plant growth requires a balanced supply of nutritional

elements. An excess of one element may result in an induced shortage of another element. Sierra Leone rice farmers are conscious of this when they say that a 'long-fallow farm' – one cleared from forest which has fallowed for 25–30 years or more – has 'too much manure', and so they delay planting the first crop of rice until as late as possible in the rainy season, when heavy rain will have dissolved some of the nitrates. Unless they do this, they say, the rice will grow over-long in the stalk and have only a small head of grain. A long-fallow farm is cultivated for 2 years, and rice yields are reputed to be much better in the second season. Grist (1975) confirms that many rice varieties respond badly to an over-supply of nitrates.

As a general rule, so Ahn (1970) notes, savanna soils tend to respond to nitrates and phosphates and forest soils to phosphates and potassium. Of the three major plant nutritional elements, then, 'phosphorus is the only one...frequently deficient in both the forest and the savanna zones of Africa' (p.167). Part of the significance of bush burning in shifting cultivation is that it helps reduce phosphorus deficiencies. Not only does burning release phosporus (and potassium) from the vegetation to the soil, but ash also temporarily raises soil pH. Phosphate is most available to plants where the soil reaction falls in the intermediate range, pH 5.5–7.0.

Soils tend to be especially acid in high rainfall districts, which explains why the Sierra Leone rice farmer is always so anxious to secure a good burn. Farmers frequently remark the correlation between poor burn and poor yields. Upland rice yields are often noticeably better in those parts of the farm where branches have been made into bonfires for piecemeal burning. Poor results on inadequately fallowed farms will be put down to the 'lightness' of the felled vegetation and the poor yield of ash.

As already noted, researchers in Nigeria in the 1930s were surprised to find that 'green manures' gave best results when cut and burnt. Samson & Crowther (1943) comment that animal manures applied to northern Nigerian soils at the low rate of c. 2.5 tonnes/ha might give better results if burnt. This suggests that West African farmers who see 'ash' as a greater priority than 'manure' may have judged their own situation correctly.

Freshly cleared soils in forest districts are often adequately supplied with nitrates, so the loss of nitrates from the burning of felled vegetation is not in itself a factor of crucial limiting significance. Due to a build-up of organic material in the soil during the dry season, nitrate levels are at their highest at the beginning of the rains. Nitrate shortages are a much more serious problem in many savanna soils, and techniques of composting, manuring, mulching, and digging-in of straw and other plant residues, tend to be much more highly developed in savanna agriculture.

In northern Nigeria, composted urban refuse and animal manure are both keenly sought after by farmers, and have become items of commerce (Hill, 1972). Farmers will negotiate for cattle herders to graze their dry season fields, and land is rented at prices reflecting the level to which it has been manured or composted. The supply of urban compost to farm villages is a major element in town–farm interaction around the larger cities of northern Nigeria (Mortimore, 1967; 1971). Permanent cultivation is the norm in the close-settled zone around these cities, but elsewhere, because demand for organic fertilizer outstrips supply, many farms are run on an infield–outfield principle, with ash, manure and compost concentrated on the best land, or on the fields closest to the settlement. This pattern of agriculture is very widely spread throughout the West African Sudan Savanna zone.

Farmers throughout West Africa commonly manage the fertility of a shifting cultivated farm through a combination of intercropping and crop rotation strategies. Intercropping is the mixing together of different crop species, or sometimes different varieties of the same crop, in a single field. The idea is to find combinations that work well together. Farmers have a number of motives in mind when intercropping: to save labour, to spread the risks of crop failure, and to limit pest and disease attack. The principles involved in intercropping are discussed more fully in Chapter 4.

Although much remains to be discovered about how intercropping systems work, it is clear that in many cases part of the benefit derives from the fact that different crops have different nutrient requirements, or that different rooting systems extract nutrients from different levels in the soil. The success of combining grain crops such as maize and sorghum with nitrogen-fixing legumes such as groundnuts and cowpeas may owe something to such factors. In the case of 'relay intercropping' – one crop in the early stages of growth while another is ripening – residues from the earlier crop may be significant in increasing the supply of nitrates to the later crop.

Farmers will also use intercropping to get the best from micro-variations in soil type within the farm field. In upland rice farms in

Sierra Leone, for example, farmers commonly use especially well-burnt patches (e.g. bonfire sites) as nurseries for new and interesting planting materials, or will use the soils at the foot of abandoned termitaria of *Macrotermes bellicosus* to plant maize and yams. Soils derived from old termite heaps often differ quite markedly from surrounding soils, both in chemical and textural properties, depending both on the depth from which the soil for the termitaria has been excavated, and the biological processes in the termite heap itself. It is not uncommon to find up to 60 abandoned *Macrotermes* heaps per hectare in Sierra Leone rice farms.

In Guinea Savanna districts, where cultivation is often continuous for several seasons, relay intercropping shades naturally into crop rotation. The basic pattern is for grain crops such as sorghum and millet to be rotated with root crops such as yam and cassava, sometimes in cycles lasting up to six or eight seasons.

Further north and south, cultivation sequences are shorter and there is less 'rotation' in the strict sense. Where cultivation lasts for two or three years continuously the cropping pattern will be changed according to a simple sequence: more demanding crops first, hardier crops later. In the Sudan Savanna zone, for example, sorghum or a sorghum/cowpea/groundnut intercrop may be followed by millet, generally reckoned to be the hardiest and least demanding of the savanna grains. In the forest zone, a farm cultivated to yam or maize in the first year may be turned over to cassava in the second, or an upland rice farm may be followed by groundnuts, cowpeas, or a groundnut/maize/cassava intercrop.

In some areas, where fallow periods have shortened due to population pressure, particular emphasis is laid on a final catch-crop (e.g. pigeon peas in the savanna or cassava in the forest) which irrespective of whether it gives an economic yield usefully 'fills in' the farm while it is in the process of reverting to bush, or helps speed up the process of fertility recovery. Pigeon pea has considerable potential in this respect, since it fixes atmospheric nitrogen, but is also extremely hardy and will grow in exhausted soils. In densely-populated parts of eastern Nigeria farmers plant their fallows with the shrub *Acioa barteri* to speed up the fallowing process (Uzozie, 1979). This idea has recently been taken up and developed at the International Institute of Tropical Agriculture in Ibadan where promising results have been obtained with *Acioa barteri* and other fallow crops in alley cropping experiments (IITA, 1981).

It is important to note that intercropping, rotations and 'pseudorotational' sequences, and catch-cropping represent some of the most important areas for innovation and experiment in West African peasant food-crop production in the twentieth century. This is not to suggest that the principles involved are in any way new in African agriculture. But farmers have recently made many useful discoveries about how to combine some of their older crops with relatively new introductions such as bitter cassava, or crops such as groundnuts for which the market has greatly expanded during the twentieth century, and so extend the useful life of shifting-cultivated farms.

Conservation and soil physical properties

Early criticisms of shifting cultivation centred on the idea that it was wasteful: it wasted vegetational resources that might be returned to the soil more effectively (if slowly and laboriously) through composting, and it exposed soil to physical damage, especially in the often steeply-dissected landscapes of the forest zone, where erosion risks were at a maximum because of steep slopes and high rainfall. If it is now apparent that shifting cultivation is often a rather effective way of mobilizing plant nutrients, then it is even more apparent that through experience of shifting cultivation farmers have developed a good understanding of soil physical properties, and that they are often rather effective at conserving these properties.

Until recently, tropical soil science has tended to neglect soil physical properties. Currently, however, it is argued (Ahn, 1970; Lal & Greenland, 1979) that soil physical properties are perhaps more crucial to sustained agricultural production in the tropics than the topic of nutrient supply which has hitherto attracted the lion's share of attention when 'fertility' issues have been under discussion. The nub of the matter is that it is easier to restore nutrients to exhausted soils than to 'rebuild' a soil that has 'collapsed' in physical terms.

Soil exposed for any length to the intense tropical rainstorms at the beginning and end of the rainy season is liable to accelerated sheet erosion. To this is added the problem of gulley erosion on steeper slopes. Not only is there overall loss of soil, and plant nutrients through erosion, but the cultivation characteristics of the soil that remains are also subject to change. Where silty material is washed out by sheet erosion then the remaining soil may become less water-retentive, and the farm more vulnerable to drought, for example.

The increased erosion risks from unwise mechanical cultivation of many West African soils are now widely appreciated. There is less appreciation that on some soils even attempts to regularize planting into rows and blocks to permit use of simple hand-operated or animal-drawn contrivances may lead to the formation of 'tractor pans' (impacted layers) under regular pathways or wheel tracks (Trouse, 1979).

Small-scale farmers in West Africa employ a wide range of techniques which are beneficial in terms of conserving soil physical properties. One of the great virtues of shifting cultivation in the forest zone is that larger trees are left *in situ* and although the lighter vegetation is brushed and burnt, the stumps and roots are not removed. This helps bind the soil, even when the first intense rainstorms fall on the freshly cultivated farm (the point at which erosion risk is at its greatest). Intercropping also facilitates protection against erosion by lengthening the period in which crops are in the farm. The diversity of plant leafing and rooting systems, and growth characteristics, in an intercropped farm also helps minimize the worst effects of rain splash. Similar effects can be obtained by mulching, which many farmers also use to conserve soil moisture during early-season periods of drought.

In savanna districts farmers make great use of heaping and ridging to create suitable soil environments for crops such as yam and sorghum. Sometimes the emphasis is on soil moisture conditions. Very large heaps are constructed in poorly-drained soils for early yam cultivation, for example. In parts of the Guinea Savanna zone, where laterite hardpan is often extensive, farmers make heaps and ridges to ensure an adequate depth of soil for plant growth without having to attempt to break up this lateritic crust. Ridging systems are often carefully 'tied' or contoured to catch soil washed off the ridges by heavy rainfall. Forest zone farmers sometimes cope with incipient erosion gullies by building simple stick bunds (Millington, 1982).

In very high rainfall districts, especially where soils are predominantly sandy or sandy loams, there is a marked tendency towards 'minimum tillage', that is disturbing the soil as little as possible in the process of cultivation. The so-called 'ploughing' of upland rice in Sierra Leone and Liberia comes into this category. Rice is first broadcast, and then lightly covered by hoeing the top inch or so of the soil. In some forest areas yams, cassava and maize may all be planted in a cleared and burnt farm without any further cultivation. This approach – the cause of many complaints (as we have seen in the case of Dudgeon) that shifting cultivators merely 'scratched the surface' of the soil, instead of 'cultivating deeply' – is now thought to have merit for soil conservation in high-rainfall areas, and research into new or modified systems of 'minimum tillage' has been actively pursued at IITA (Lal, 1979a; 1979b).

In summary, then, it is apparent that 'shifting cultivation' in West Africa, far from encouraging a wasteful attitude to soil resources, has provided farmers with a good, practical, education in the more important principles of soil management. From the point of view of fertilization, modern soil science confirms the validity of the forest farmer's emphasis on 'ash' and the savanna farmer's emphasis on 'manure' and 'compost'. From the point of view of soil conserva-tion, there is no lack of evidence for the view that the West African cultivator is well-abreast of many of the key issues. If the experience of shifting cultivation has tended to emphasize the importance of soil physical properties in the maintenance of sustained yields, modern soil science confirms that this emphasis is well-placed.

Ahn (1970: 150) notes that 'in popular literature and some introductory books and articles it is often implied that one has merely to apply fertilizers to a soil in order to get better crops'. Development projects in West Africa all too frequently appear to operate on this basis, supplying farmers with a 'recommended' fertilizer, and a minimum of general guidance for its use. But as Ahn notes, the problem is rarely so simple. Disappointing results with fertilizers in many areas stem from the fact that farmers are given them much as a doctor prescribes a drug. Extension advice sometimes makes the parallel explicit: here is 'medicine' for the soil. Local conditions vary too much for the 'prescription' approach to work effectively. Better use of fertilizer requires a much more open-ended approach, with, in all probability, farmers doing much of the necessary experimentation for themselves.

A thorough understanding of the legacy of shifting cultivation in West African farming systems suggests that the right kinds of skills and experience to sustain such experiments are already present and widespread among small-scale cultivators. Rather than concentrate on selling a 'package' of soil 'medicine' to farmers, the challenge for 'populist' agricultural development is to establish a thoroughgoing and self-sustaining programme of improved soil management drawing strength and initial impetus from the skills, experience and experimental ability already present within the farming community.

3 The ecology of West African farming systems

II Intercropping and wet-land agriculture

Two areas of agricultural ecology where West African small-holders have displayed special enterprise and inventiveness are intercropping and the effective use of wet-land environments. For a long time agricultural researchers and outside commentators on African agriculture failed to recognize the significance of indigenous developments in these two areas. In extreme cases it was suggested that intercropping was further evidence of the intrinsic 'backwardness' of African agriculture, and that West Africa, in contrast to most parts of Asia, had no history or tradition of 'irrigation'. Recent work has helped to rectify some of these misconceptions.

Intercropping

Intercropping is rare or unknown in temperate zone agriculture. In West Africa, by contrast, 80 per cent of all farm land is intercropped. Not only is intercropping dominant throughout the region but it is also a theme upon which small-scale farmers have quietly elaborated many new and interesting variations in recent years. Quite rightly, the topic of intercropping has now begun to attract the scientific attention its regional preponderance so clearly demands (Belshaw, 1979; Igbozurike, 1971a; 1971b; 1977; Steiner, 1982).

Terminology

Intercropping – the planting of different crops in the same field during the same season – is used synonymously with the term 'mixed cropping'. Where a crop is planted and harvested, and followed by further crops in the same year, it is usual to speak of 'sequential cropping'. The term 'relay cropping' is used where these sequences overlap. Intercropping, sequential cropping and relay cropping are thus distinguished from 'sole cropping' – the planting of one crop per field per season, and 'monoculture' – the planting of a single crop in the same field for a succession of seasons, or indefinitely (Steiner, 1982).

Variables
Intercropping systems can vary in four main ways:

1 In terms of the number of crops and crop-combinations involved. In the forest zone up to 60 crop species may be planted in one farm, though 20–30 is probably nearer the norm. Numbers of crop species tend to be lower in savanna intercropped farms – typically 10–15. In both forest and savanna areas each intercropped farm will be dominated by a handful of main crops: e.g. a major staple, or a combination of two or three main food and cash crops. Combinations of crops vary according to local environmental, economic and social conditions. In the forest zone the scope for variation in crop combinations is almost infinite. Even in the savanna, there is much scope for varying combinations to suit local conditions. Norman (1974) found as many as 147 distinct intercrop combinations in three villages in the Zaria region in northern Nigeria.

2 In terms of patterns of ownership and labour responsibilities. On farms in the yam cultivation zone from Ivory Coast to eastern Nigeria it is common to find that men own and carry out the bulk of the work on the main crop – white yam – but that women own and are responsible for the subsidiary intercrops, e.g. maize, coco-yam, cassava, and vegetables (see, for example, Uzozie, 1979). Similar patterns of social specialization are also found further west, where rice takes over from yam and cassava as the dominant staple. On rice farms in Sierra Leone (Richards, 1985), for example, the 'head of household' (whether a man or woman) has a major responsibility for the upland rice crop, whereas the subsidiary crops (e.g. swamp rice, cotton, beniseed, sorghum, root crops and vegetables) belong to other members of the household (wives, senior women, 'juniors'). Intercropping practices are much influenced, therefore, by social factors – e.g. the number of dependents per household. It is essential that proposed changes in intercropping systems take into account such social variables.

3 In terms of spatial organization. Intercropping may be carried

out according to some regular layout, e.g. a definite planting sequence along a cultivation ridge, a suite of plants specific to cultivation mounds (a pattern common in yam-cultivation districts), or regular alternation of crops by rows. Regular patterns of this sort are common in savanna districts, and are fairly easily modified to permit simple mechanization. In forest districts, intercropping is more often entirely random. This is a consequence of the fact that brushed farms are rarely if ever completely cleared or stumped, and that in the case of upland rice farms many of the intercrops are sown by broadcasting along with the rice. Where farmers match specific crops to micro-level differences in soil types within a single farm, this is sometimes referred to as 'patchwork' intercropping. The vertical dimension is also important (Steiner, 1982). In forest districts it is possible to work out sequences mixing field and tree crops. 'Multistorey' intercropping is especially advantageous in terms of erosion control, though it tends to exacerbate problems caused by low levels of solar radiation.

4 In terms of timing. The farmer manipulates three variables: planting date, maturity period and harvest date. Skilful scheduling – e.g. planting quick and long-maturing varieties together, or staggering planting so that different crops ripen together – achieves a number of desirable results: a supply of foodstuffs during the 'hungry gap' prior to the main harvest, minimization of 'storage losses' by extending the harvest over as long a period as possible, and elimination of labour bottlenecks, at planting or harvest for example.

Local and regional variations in intercropping practices

Although intercropping is important in small-scale cultivation throughout West Africa, four major types of local and regional variation have been observed.

1 The significance of intercropping tends to be at a maximum in the forest zone, where the range of possible crop combinations is greatest.

2 Intercropping tends to be more elaborate and intensive on farm plots close to the settlement than on more distant fields (it is common sense not to have to pay a great deal of attention or carry the bulkiest inputs to the most inaccessible fields).

3 In some regions the more complex systems of intercropping are associated with more fertile soils.

4   In other regions the intensity of intercropping – both in terms of the number of different crops included in a mixture, and in terms of planting densities – correlates with population density.

It has been suggested (Morgan, 1955; Lagemann, 1977; Uzozie, 1979) that in eastern Nigeria, intensified intercropping on permanently cultivated, manured and composted 'infield' farms is one of the ways in which farmers have responded to land shortages over the last 50–75 years or so. Opinions vary as to the success of this response. Igbozurike (1977) and Uzozie (1979) regard these adjustments in an optimistic light. Others (cf. Lagemann, 1977) incline more to the view that they are 'involutionary' – that farmers are working harder to achieve the same results. It must be stressed, however, that the density of population in central-eastern Nigeria is untypical of West Africa as a whole. This would seem to rule out the involutionary hypothesis as an explanation of the general importance of intercropping. The near universality of intercropping throughout West Africa must, as Samson & Crowther (1943: 36) noted, be 'strong presumptive evidence of some direct benefit'.

Benefits from intercropping
Farmers see a wide range of advantages in intercropping:

Better and more reliable yields
In many cases yields from intercropping surpass those from sole cropping systems (Ajibola Taylor, 1977; Baker & Yusuf, 1976). In other cases the principal appeal is that of greater reliability (Gebrekidan, 1976; Kayumbo, 1976). From the perspective of the small-scale farmer facing an uncertain environment, reliability of yield is an especially important characteristic. West African farmers tend to choose to minimize risks in preference to maximizing profits. This means choosing to plant a crop or combination of crops with a lower average yield but which keeps close to this average even in the worst years, rather than one with a higher long-term average but which drops far below that average in a poor year. Where a farmer in Europe borrows from the bank to tide him over a bad year and prepares for better results next time, the West African farmer may not survive to try again. Results from throughout the tropics now confirm that intercropping is especially important in levelling out yield fluctuations (Table 3; Figure 5).

Table 3 *Yield fluctuations with intercropping*

	Coefficients of variation (for three years and three replicates)	
	Average for crops grown singly	Crop associations
Cassava/bean	33.04	27.54
Cassava/sweet potato	23.87	13.42
Cassava/maize/sweet potato	31.05	21.44
Cassava/maize/bean	25.04	14.95

Source: Steiner (1982: 95) citing Moreno & Hart (1979).

A smoother labour input profile
Due to relatively low population densities and recent selective loss of young people through rural out-migration (Zachariah & Condé, 1981), it is common for farmers in many parts of West Africa to suffer from labour shortages. Even where labour is not in short supply overall, it is helpful to be able to arrange the farm so that tasks present themselves in a steady and readily manageable way over the duration of the farming season.

The size and productivity of a farm enterprise will be limited by the amount of labour the farmer can mobilize to cope with the most

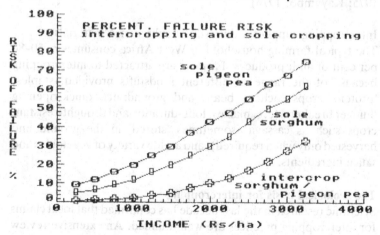

Figure 5   Yield stability of sorghum/pigeon pea intercrops in India
Source: Rao & Willey (1980) cited in Steiner (1982).

labour-demanding task (the 'labour bottleneck'). Many intended 'improvements' in West African farming systems, especially those involving mechanization, solve one bottleneck, e.g. constraints on the size of farm one household can cultivate – only to create further bottlenecks later in the year, e.g. at weeding time (Karimu & Richards, 1980). By contrast, a study by Diehl (1981) of farming systems in central Nigeria shows in detail the way in which 'traditional' intercropping strategies help flatten out the labour input profile; extending the planting season, staggering the harvest and filling in 'slack' periods. When women broadcast cotton and other intercrops on upland rice farms in Sierra Leone, the only additional labour input is the effort required for harvesting, since the crops are planted and weeded along with the main rice crop (Richards, 1985).

Better control of pests, weeds and diseases
At one level this is largely a matter of effective use of labour. All crops are weeded in one operation. Competition from quick-growing minor crops may keep weeds down in the early part of the season to the benefit of a slower-growing main crop. A single intercropped plot is much easier to protect against birds, rodents and human thieves than several sole-cropped plots. It is also suggested that intercropping is less vulnerable to pest, weed and disease attack because of its greater ecological diversity (Norton, 1975; Kayumbo, 1976).

Intercropping supplies a diversity of subsistence materials
The typical farming household in West Africa consumes c. 50–80 per cent of all it produces. Farmers are attracted to intercropping because of the range of different foodstuffs provided: staples, 'protein' crops such as beans and groundnuts, quick-ripening 'hunger breakers' (e.g. maize), long-duration and drought-resistant crops such as cassava (sometimes 'stored' in the ground and harvested only when required), and a wide variety of vegetables and sauce ingredients.

The ecological basis for intercropping
Scientific research in the last decade has confirmed that local claims for intercropping practices are well founded. An extensive review of the literature by Steiner (1982) brings out the significance of the following factors:

1   Successful intercropping involves spatial and temporal complementarities. Cereals (e.g. maize and sorghum) and legumes such as cow peas and groundnuts work well in combination because the legumes root much more deeply than the cereals, and this leads, overall, to better exploitation of 'mobile' resources such as nitrates and soil moisture. Better uptake of plant nutrients and soil moisture is also achieved where a quick and a slow-maturing variety of the same crop (or similar crops) are planted together, because the two varieties put major demands on resources at different times. Andrews (1972) reports an 80 per cent yield advantage where 85-day millet and 150-day sorghum are intercropped. In the case of sorghum, Baker (1979) claims clear gains to intercropping where the difference in height between varieties is more than 59 cm and the difference in harvest dates is more than 51 days. For this latter reason, it is doubtful whether any advantage could be obtained from intercropping where the rainy season is very short (3–4 months). This helps explain the relative lack of significance of intercropping in some parts of the Sahel.

2   Better aggregate yields from crop mixtures involving legumes are thought to reflect, to some degree, the fact that leguminous plants are able to 'fix' atmospheric nitrogen through their root nodules. This benefits later crops in a 'relay' sequence, but the notion that intercropped legumes directly assist in the 'fertilization' of adjacent contemporary crops is open to doubt. More generally, there is evidence that later crops in a sequence, or slower maturing crops, benefit from the breakdown of residues from earlier crops, and that intercropping systems may be able to make especially efficient use of fertilizer applications (see below).

3   A well-designed intercropping system achieves beneficial results through its impact on soil temperatures and micro-climate. Some crops benefit from conditions of increased humidity and reduction of soil temperature and transpiration adjacent to earlier established, leafy, plants. Other crops benefit from the wind break effect provided by tree crops (e.g. the baobab and shea butter trees common in many savanna farms) or by a boundary 'hedge' of tall grain such as sorghum. Farmers have to exercise considerable care, however, to reduce competition for light in intercropped farms. Some crops, and some varieties, are better adapted than others to shady conditions. Cocoyam, cowpea and yam are often successful under shade, but maize and cassava need much more open conditions.

4 Competition between crops in an intercropping system tends to exclude or minimize weed problems, and a diversity of crops and crop varieties helps keep down explosive population increase of insect pests or the epidemic spread of plant diseases, where pests and diseases are species- or variety-specific. On the other hand, the intercropped farm is not a very 'clean' environment. In fact, its great ecological variety helps keep alive many pests and pathogens, although at individually low levels of activity. It is a controversial point in ecology, therefore, whether it is better to aim to eliminate completely these sources of infection, but with the risk that if the pest or pathogen should recur the damage might be on a devastating scale, or whether the endemic low level 'infection' characteristic of intercropping is preferable on the grounds that it stimulates immune responses (in this case, plants and cultivation techniques adapted to a certain amount of regular damage). Evidence that a low level of deliberate infestation with spider mites of the genus *Tetranychus* stimulates such an 'immune response' in cotton is reported by Karban & Carey (1984), though little is yet known about how plants are able to protect themselves in this way.

Intercropping: a route to an indigenous agricultural revolution?
Recent research makes two points which help explain the great significance of intercropping throughout West Africa. Intercropping systems are best adapted to soils of low and indifferent fertility. Compared with sole cropping systems, the percentage gains from intercropping are greater on soils of lower rather than higher fertility. The second point is that optimum planting densities tend to be higher for intercropping systems than they would be for comparable sole cropping systems. A degree of 'crowding' seems to stimulate intercropped plants to perform better. Thus intercropping is a viable route to better yields both in areas of land shortage such as eastern Nigeria and parts of northern Nigeria and also in areas, so typical of much of rural West Africa, where low population density correlates with low soil fertility.

It might be better to view intercropping, therefore, not as a set of 'traditional' techniques, but as evidence of progress towards an agricultural revolution well-adapted to West African conditions (Igbozurike, 1977). The idea that West African farmers might already be well on the way towards an agricultural revolution of their own devising has a parallel in the history of English farming. Kerridge (1967), in a major if controversial historical study, argues that innovations normally associated with the so-called 'agricultural revolution' of the eighteenth century in large measure had been developed and put into 'running order' at an earlier period by ordinary farmers without access to (or need of) means of publicizing their experiments and innovations. The main sense, he suggests, in which there was an 'agricultural revolution' in the eighteenth century was that this was the point at which many of the agricultural issues and innovations of the previous two centuries came into public and literary focus. This focus was provided by skilled writers, such as Arthur Young (Mingay, 1975), who acted as propagandists for many of these changes, and by the emergence of an agricultural science capable of supplying theoretically-based explanations of the principles underlying innovations that had been found to work. But it is important to note that science followed rather than led this revolution. It would seem that exactly the same thing has happened in the case of intercropping (Belshaw, 1979; Monyo, Ker & Campbell, 1976; Okigbo & Greenland, 1976).

Viewed correctly, I would argue, intercropping should be seen as an area where West African smallholders have concentrated much experimental initiative and invention. This approach is dynamic and inventive, not traditional and time-bound. Steiner (1982) provides an excellent example. Recent FAO fertilizer trials in Plateau State of Nigeria compared fertilizer use on sole crop and

Table 4 *Yields with and without intercropping* (Plateau State, Nigeria)

	Value–cost ratios	
	Fertilizer + farmers' cultivation practices	*Fertilizer + 'improved' cultivation practices*
Monocrop		
Sorghum	5.6	10.2
Maize	4.1	12.2
Intercrop		
Maize/sorghum	20.2	17.7
Yam/maize	77.3	24.6
Sorghum/cowpea	13.5	8.4

Source: Steiner (1982: 135), citing FAO (1979)

intercropped farms, under both the farmer's own and a set of 'improved' management practices. Where sole cropping was tried, 'improved' management practices gave better returns (value-cost ratios) than local practices. The position was sharply reversed for intercropping. Table 4 shows a thought-provoking set of results. The best returns were for a 'modern' input, applied on intercropped farms, but using *local* management procedures. It is precisely on evidence of this sort: the ability of West African small-holders to get best results from a combination of (so-called) 'modern' and 'traditional' techniques, that the case for the 'populist' strategy rests. Science (and this I go on to argue much more fully in Chapters 5 and 6) should be the servant not the master of this kind of inventiveness.

Wet-land agriculture in West Africa

Another area where West African small-holders have been especially inventive is in the use of wet-land. Water-control measures are few, because when labour is in short supply it makes sense to work with, rather than to override, the natural rise and fall of rivers and streams. Water-control measures are almost invariably labour intensive.

Wet-land specialists are found only in a few relatively restricted localities: for instance the Inland Delta of the Niger in Mali, the flood plains of the larger rivers in the Sudan and Sahel Savanna Zones (e.g. the Hadejia and Sokoto Rivers in northern Nigeria), and the estuarine swamps of the Upper Guinea coast (from Casamance in Senegal to Turner's Peninsula in Sierra Leone). Elsewhere, many farmers (perhaps the majority) supplement a main rain-fed farm with some element of wet-land cultivation, e.g. cultivation of valley-bottom soils during the dry season.

If it was a long time before science took proper note of intercropping, African wet-land cultivation techniques have been even less 'visible' on the horizons of planners and policy makers. Up until about 1970 'irrigation' meant large-scale irrigation, equivalent in scale, and sometimes in lack of effectiveness, to the ill-fated mechanization schemes discussed in Chapter 1. This was a trend affecting all developing countries. Stern (1980: 22) notes:

By a curious anomaly the twenty years between 1950 and 1970 which saw so many disappointments in irrigation at field and farm level also saw an increase of seventy per cent in the areas of land under irrigation in developing countries, representing very substantial capital investments in new works.

Since then, attitudes have changed quite markedly, and much more attention is now given in agencies such as FAO and the World Bank to the irrigation needs and interests of the small farmer. Even so, it is still common to find that the only types of 'irrigation' to register with planners are labour-intensive systems with water-control. Stern's admirable manual of small-scale irrigation techniques takes a different view, however.

Irrigation is any process, other than natural precipitation, which supplies water to crops…[and includes] run-off farming, humid culture, and micro and manual irrigation, because these are important and significant features of small scale development (Stern, 1980:3).

By this definition, irrigation is already widespread in West Africa. A review by Underhill (1984) lists eleven distinct types of small-scale irrigation system in Africa, nine of which are dependent on gravity (Table 5). The major techniques are estuarine cultivation, flood-plain and valley-bottom farming (including flood-retreat and flood-advance methods), and run-off (seep zone) cultivation. The integrated use of wetlands and uplands across the valley profile is sometimes termed 'catenary cultivation'.

A number of West African countries have experienced schemes to introduce small farmers to water-controlled irrigation techniques based on South or South-East Asian models. These often prove too labour-intensive for local conditions. A better approach may be to concentrate on the extension and improvement of irrigation techniques indigenous to West Africa (Richards, 1985; cf. Scudder, 1980; Underhill, 1984).

Estuarine cultivation
Temne enterprise in opening up the mangrove swamps of the estuaries of the Great and Little Scarcies to meet the demands of the growing market for rice in late nineteenth century Freetown has already been mentioned in Chapter 1 as a good example of indigenous capacity for innovation in the food-crop sector in West African agriculture.

Rice cultivation in mangrove swamps is practised quite widely along the coasts of Guinea and Guinea-Bissau, and it is possible that cultivators along the Scarcies first learnt the necessary skills from the Baga people of Guinea. Opening up a mangrove swamp farm requires very considerable labour inputs for the initial clearing (it is worth noting that the surrounding districts are among the most heavily-populated in Sierra Leone). After clearing, however, the farm is available for permanent cultivation, since it is fertilized afresh each year by material brought down by the rainy season flood.

During the dry season the mangrove mud flats are flooded each

Table 5 *Types of small-scale irrigation found in Africa*

Small-scale irrigation in Africa

Classification of typical physical systems

---

1 River floodplain or extensive plains that can be commanded from a river: (i) gravity, (ii) pumped
2 Seasonally deep-flooded lands for floating rice
3 Seasonally shallow-flooded lands for rice (and other crops on mounds)
4 Recession irrigation – deltas, large seasonally-flooded plains, reservoirs
5 Mangrove/coastal swamps: gravity and pumped
6 Inland Valley Swamps or *Bas fonds*, typically 5–100 ha, long and narrow, in hilly areas: gravity
7 Bolilands – wide flat saucer-shaped depressions with poor drainage: gravity
8 Small areas commanded by furrows from a stream in hilly country: gravity
9 Arid areas:
   a gravity, lifted or pumped from seasonal rivers
   b gravity by bunding (rainfall retention and water harvesting)
   c pumped or lifted from shallow wells
10 Spate irrigation using flash floods: gravity
11 Groundwater development (i) from medium to deep aquifers (ii) from shallow wells: pumped or lifted

---

Source: Underhill (1984)

day by salty tides. As the rainy season progresses, however, the daily tidal flood turns from salt water to fresh. By August the soils are washed free of salt and it is possible to transplant rice on to land previously prepared by two hoeings (Gwynne-Jones, Mitchell, Harvey & Swindell, 1977). Regular flooding limits weed growth. It will be recalled from discussion in Chapter 1, that this local technique, using 'natural and unrestricted irrigation by tidal river water' proved much more effective than the wartime polder irrigation scheme at Rokupr and elsewhere along the Sierra Leone coast, suggesting that farmers' preferences for 'natural' irrigation methods are often well-founded.

According to Glanville (1938) Scarcies farmers had made considerable efforts to find the best rice varieties suited to these conditions. The Agriculture Department assisted this process by introducing a number of exotic varieties, including 'floating' rices from India and Indo-China, and by operating a successful 'revolving seed scheme'. This scheme (noted in Chapter 1) distributed 93,000 bushels of 'improved' seed for swamp cultivation from 1935 onwards, and was terminated in 1947 having achieved its purpose of 'getting large supplies of improved varieties into general use' (Annual Report, Department of Agriculture, 1948: 3). Several of these varieties are now widespread throughout Sierra Leone, and have assumed local names.

Flood-plain and valley-bottom cultivation

The idea of water control on minor streams for irrigation purposes has a number of theoretical advantages, and has been pushed quite strongly in some countries as an innovation of potential interest to small-scale farmers. A basic 'model' for rice cultivation envisages that the valley bottom should be levelled, and head bund, main channel and side channels constructed to carry the water round the farm. No provision is made for water storage.

Unfortunately theory and practice do not necessarily coincide (Plate 1). West African rivers and streams are strongly seasonal. Even in forested districts it is common for all but the larger streams to dry up during the dry season. During the rainy season streams may be subject to large variations in rates and depth of flow. Many West African valley soils are too poor and sandy to support high yields under continuous cropping. These are all factors that condemn farmers to heavy constructional expenditures, uncertain yields, or both (Lappia, 1980).

Doubts about the economic viability of water-controlled valley swamp cultivation in West African conditions date back to work by an American team in Liberia in the middle 1950s (Buchanan, Prejean, Girardot & Harris, 1956). One of the conclusions of this study was that in order to get an economic crop of rice it would be

Plate 1 Unsuccessful swamp farm

necessary to abandon transplanting and reduce bunding and ditching to a bare minimum. Their proposal, in effect, amounts to the 're-invention' of an approach to rice cultivation in inland valley swamps already widespread throughout the West African rice zone.

In Sierra Leone, many (perhaps the majority) of farm households plant a small amount of rice in such swamps, and sometimes along the actual water course itself. The work is additional to that on the main 'upland' rice farm (the 'household' farm), and is undertaken by women and young dependent males, especially in order to secure an individual income. As personal business it must not interfere with the work of the main household farm, so techniques employed are labour-saving in the extreme. In these circumstances farmers prefer to manage valley-bottom land by selecting 'floating' or flood-tolerant varieties capable of adjusting to variable flood depths in preference to laborious water-control.

In northern Sierra Leone, where upland soils tend to be of low fertility and population densities are quite high, swamp cultivation is more frequently an integral element in the 'household' farm. Typically, valley bottom land will comprise a quarter or a third of the whole enterprise, but because of better yields than on uplands, may supply a household with more than a half of its rice. Valley rice cultivation in these circumstances frequently involves some element of water-control. Only rarely, however, will a farm be completely levelled. The tendency is to construct numerous low bunds following the contour. Several land facets with distinct water regimes are created thereby. The upper bunded facets are watered by run-off rather than stream flow. Farmers exploit these varied facets by carefully matching rice types to specific soil moisture conditions. Individual farmers may plant up to 8–10 different varieties per farm, and 25–50 different varieties might be in use in a single village at any one point in time. Similar techniques of valley management have been described for rice farmers in Casamance in Senegal. Here, however, farmers devote most or all of their time to irrigated agriculture (Linares, 1970; 1981).

The typical 'household' farm in northern Sierra Leone (Spencer, 1975), comprising two-thirds upland rice and one-third swamp rice grown according to valley land-utilization practices of the kind just described, has a flatter labour input profile across the year than farms based entirely on upland cultivation or 'improved' practices of swamp cultivation (Figure 6). As noted in the case of intercrop-

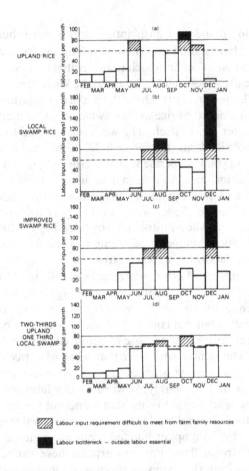

Figure 6 Labour input bottlenecks, swamp and upland rice farming in N. Sierra Leone

ping, small-scale farmers are especially keen to avoid labour bottlenecks, since these either constrain output or compel labour hiring. Not only do farmers in northern Sierra Leone have little cash to invest in labour, but as is common in many societies where only a small percentage of total farm labour ever comes to market, prices for hired labour tend to be unrealistically high (cf. Kula, 1976).

'Improved' valley cultivation practices, of the kind promoted by the World Bank-funded Integrated Agricultural Development Projects in Sierra Leone, are not readily combined with existing cultivation practices. The trouble in this case is that the 'swamp loan package' is fixed and indivisible in size. Local valley management practices are much more flexible so it is far easier for the individual farmer to 'programme' the right mix of swamp and upland to suit household or individual requirements. (I have often seen swamp plots of no more than a few metres square made by pre-teenage children.) From the outset, the 'improved' valley farming package has been designed as a *replacement* for upland cultivation. Local demand is for a farming system *combining* these two land-use types.

A further disadvantage of 'improved' swamp rice cultivation systems, as so far presented by development agencies to the West African farmer, is that they make no provision for intercropping. Where swamp rice cultivation has been elaborated by local initiative it is common to find that some element of intercropping has been introduced. Farmers may experiment with mixtures of quick and long-duration rice varieties, or with cropping sequences in which the main rice crop is followed by a dry-season crop of sweet potatoes, tobacco, groundnuts or cassava. In the Uboma Rural Development Project in central-eastern Nigeria, some farmers have turned their back on rice sole cropping as recommended by the project (Lagemann, 1977) and have experimented with ridged swamps, in which rice is planted down flooded furrows and cassava and cocoyams are intercropped on the ridges (Plate 2).

Dry-season cultivation in valley-bottom lands is widespread throughout West Africa (Richards, 1983). In northern Nigeria valley land of this sort is known (in Hausa) as **fadama** , and may be planted to rice in the wet season and to crops such as wheat, tobacco, onions and tomatoes during the dry season (Goddard, Fine & Norman, 1971). Sometimes, exploitation of residual moisture in hydromorphic soils is supplemented by **shadoof** (bucket) irrigation. **Fadama** cultivation, like valley rice cultivation in central and southern Sierra Leone, is mainly a matter for individuals rather than the household. It is a way of earning a cash income in the 'slack' season, and is thus equivalent to seasonal labour migration to town, or to the cocoa belt of western Nigeria.

Where river flood plains are unusually extensive – notably, the Inland Delta of the Niger and the valley of the Hadejia River in Hadejia Emirate, north-east of Kano – valley cultivation is a full-time enterprise, and complex systems of flood-advance and flood-retreat agriculture have been developed. The degree of botanical and ecological skill displayed by farmers in the Inland

Plate 2. 'Intercropped swamp' at Uboma

Delta in matching varieties and planting strategies to the rise and fall of the annual flood is well-illustrated in studies by Gallais (1967) and Harlan & Pasquereau (1969).

Farmers in the the Hadejia Valley plant rice during the rainy season on shallow-flooding **fadama** land and cotton on intervening bars. Dyking is used to protect the rice against undue flooding and channel irrigation supplies river water to the cotton. During the dry season, vegetables, tobacco and wheat utilize residual moisture, in some cases supplemented by **shadoof** irrigation. The Hadejia Valley once supplied about two-thirds of all the cotton and rice produced in Kano State and much of the wheat and vegetable supply for Kano markets. The system began to fail in the early 1970s more, Stock (1978) argues, because of the disruption of the downstream water regime through the construction of the Tiga Dam, than as a result of the 'Sahel Drought'. Downstream disruption of indigenous irrigation systems is a common adverse consequence of large-scale dam construction throughout Africa (Adeniyi, 1973; Scudder, 1980).

Run-off (seep-zone) agriculture
Many West African small-holders obtain valuable early season crops by exploiting the lower part of the valley slope. In many cases the soils involved are true valley-bottom soils subject to regular flooding (hydromorphic soils). In other cases however, the niche the farmer exploits (a river terrace or former levee, perhaps) stands above the flood plain proper. In such situations the soils gain much of their early moisture (and fertility) by trapping run-off from the higher reaches of the valley profile rather than from the rising river flood.

The distinction is a fine one, admittedly, but worth making since management practices and problems in the 'run-off zone' are often quite distinct from those on the valley floor proper. Valley-bottom soils often tend to have a high clay content. Soils in the run-off zone are frequently silty. Silts are sometimes better than clays for early season cultivation since they yield their water to plants more readily. At the same time, however, they are subject to quite high erosion risks, especially at the point where a river terrace or levee makes its final drop to the valley floor. Careful management is required, and it is here that Sierra Leone rice farmers, for example, concentrate attention given to erosion control (e.g. construction of stick bunds across incipient gulleys: Plate 3). Erosion higher up the slope may be ignored, or even welcomed as part of the process of

Plate 3   Construction of stick bunds across incipient gulleys

enriching run-off zone soils. This is why a run-off plot makes especially good sense when linked to an upland farm. Farms on true hydromorphic soils are more frequently separate.

Nigerian yam farmers frequently make farms for early yams in the run-off zone (Atteh, 1980). Diehl (1981), working in three villages in the Niger-Benue confluence region, has demonstrated a number of important complementarities between 'early season' farms of this sort and the main farm. Yam farmers derive a disproportionate part of their cash income from sales from these farms, because the crop is ready when prices are at their highest. In addition, early season farms supply planting materials for the main farm and help smooth out labour bottleneck problems.

The run-off zone is often important in Sierra Leone rice farming as the location for quick-ripening rices planted a month or two ahead of the main upland crop. Quick-ripening varieties (of less than 100 days duration) planted in the run-off zone can be harvested at the height of the pre-harvest hunger period in July/August, a month or two in advance of the upland harvest and a full three months ahead of rice planted in valley swamps. Research and commercial attention has been concentrated on the heavy-yielding, long-duration, swamp rices. Work with quick rices in the run-off zone has attracted less attention because yields appear to be low. Some of the earliest experiments at Njala (in 1912) concerned an 85-day African rice (*Oryza glaberrima*) known in Mende as **pende**, a variety frequently planted by local farmers in the run-off zone. Work on **pende** was abandoned because yields were only *c.* 400–500 kg/ha (compared with typical yields for upland and swamp rices of 1000 kg/ha and 1500–2000 kg/ha respectively). The decision to ignore **pende**, and run-off zone cultivation more generally, failed to take account, however, of the fact that rice prices in June–July– August are often double the price prevailing when the long- duration swamp varieties are ready for harvest (in November– December, after the main upland harvest is complete).

As the Njala soil scientist H.W. Dougall noted (Chapter 1), run-off zone soils are also especially important as sites for rice nurseries. When farmers carry out their own experiments and trials (see Chapter 6) it is typically in the run-off zone that they begin. Clearly, then, run-off zone agriculture should be high on the agenda of any 'populist' programme for agricultural development in West Africa. Its past neglect by research institutions is symptomatic of the gap separating the perceptions and priorities of farmers and 'formal sector' researchers.

Conclusion

This and the previous chapter have argued that small-scale farmers in West Africa have already laid some of the foundations for an indigenous agricultural revolution. 'Shifting cultivation' is by no means solely a 'problem'. It may also be viewed as a resource – as a 'field laboratory' where farmers have gained a wealth of ecological experience and expertise (in soil management, for example). Development programmes might aim to make better use than at present of skills thus acquired. In intercropping and effective use of valley land without need for expensive water lifting or storage devices, West African farmers have pioneered where formal agricultural science now follows. Past failure to support indigenous intitiatives in these areas has had profound consequences for the present food production crisis in the region.

4 The ecological dynamics of West African food-crop farming systems:
Two case studies

Planners and policy makers frequently underestimate capacity for change in the peasant farming sector, because it is difficult for them to spot and assess significant developments when these are spread over a large number of small-scale production units. In these conditions each change may be small in itself but the cumulative effect of great significance. Innovation in the peasant food-crop production sector is especially likely to escape wider notice. Where small-scale farmers have figured at all on the planning horizon, it is as producers of 'export' crops. Food production by small-holders tends to be dismissed as 'subsistence' farming, with the assumption that it is 'traditional', and therefore 'timeless' and 'changeless'.

In Chapter 2 it was suggested that this apparent 'invisibility' of change in peasant farming was compounded by ecological conditions in West Africa, where tropical diversity is further heightened by the absence of labour-intensive modifications of the landscape of the kind found in regions of higher population density. Farming systems may be quite different in localities only 10–20 km apart. In the most highly diversified landscapes (e.g. parts of the Jos Plateau) specific agricultural settings may be exploited by, perhaps, as few as a 100 or so farm households (Netting, 1968; Sharpe, 1983). Even in more uniform environments – the Hausa plains of northern Nigeria, for example – the notion of 'standard' land-use combinations and farming systems begins to break down at the regional level (cf. significant differences in farming practices reported for Kano, Katsina, Sokoto and Zaria, by Hill, 1972; 1977; Norman, 1967; Goddard, Fine & Norman, 1971).

The present chapter looks at two West African food-production systems, one in Sierra Leone, the other in Nigeria. Both are examples of successful exploitation by small-holders of highly specific sets of environmental conditions. The first case-study – rice production in central Sierra Leone – is intended to exemplify the development of food-production systems in regions with low population density and low rates of rural population increase. The second case-study – the combined development of root-crop and palm-oil production in an area on the southern fringes of the 'cocoa belt' in western Nigeria – illustrates changes characteristic of regions with higher densities and rates of population increase. Two main arguments are supported: first, that invention, exploration, and adaptation in West African peasant farming are as marked a feature of the low population density region as they are of the region of high population density; and second that the degree of specificity in the farming systems in these areas is such as to bring into question the relevance and feasibility of conventional 'input package' approaches to rural development.

The first point suggests that 'population pressure' (as envisaged by Boserup, 1965; 1980; Wilkinson, 1973) is far from being a unique or specially significant stimulus to grass-roots change. The second point underlines the need for major reorientation of agricultural research and development strategies. It is unlikely that there will ever be sufficient funds to mount specific research programmes for each of West Africa's specialized farming ecologies. The suggestion, further developed in Chapter 6, is for more support to be directed to the continuation of R & D work which farmers already, in effect, undertake for themselves (cf. Howes & Chambers, 1979; Biggs & Clay, 1981). This is why the case-studies in the current chapter lay especial emphasis on the ways in which farmers explore their environment, invent new techiques, and figure out innovative approaches to both familiar and unprecedented problems.

Rice farming and wet-land management in central Sierra Leone

The Annual Report of the Sierra Leone Department of Agriculture for 1936 drew attention to a surprising set of statistics. Although world prices for palm produce, Sierra Leone's major agricultural export, collapsed in 1929, in each succeeding year the Sierra Leone government railway recorded a sizeable increase in railings of food crops. This appears to have been part of a more general switch into food crops at the time. In 1934 (at the height of the recession) Sierra Leone exported more than 1000 tons of rice (in most years from 1919 onwards the country was just barely self-sufficient, or as in

1919 itself, suffered quite severe rice shortages). And yet any link between decline in tree-crop exports and changes in the food crop sector was far from direct, since further investigation showed that whereas the majority of tree-crop exports came from the Eastern Province all of the increase in food-crop railings originated in the Southern Province, from stations between Mano and Mabang (Figure 7).

Quite how the recession triggered an apparent upsurge in foodstuff production for market is not yet clear. What is striking, however, is that the area from which the increased food-crop railings originated has long been considered relatively 'backward' in agricultural terms. More specifically, the Southern Province had (and has) the lowest percentage of land devoted to swamp rice of all three provinces in Sierra Leone, and has been the area where 'improved' (i.e. water-controlled) swamp rice farming has made least headway (Johnny, 1979). Here, then, we have an interesting paradox. Farmers with a reputation for clinging to 'outmoded' techniques were, in the 1930s, among the vanguard of those responding to new market demands and opportunities in food-crop agriculture.

It is worthwhile, therefore, to look more closely at the region from which these foodstuff railings derived. Mano was the station contributing the biggest share (Figure 7). Njala, the headquarters of

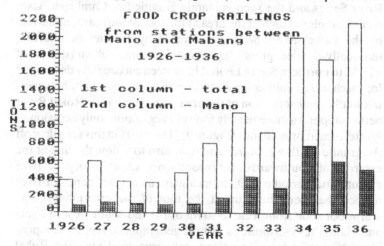

Figure 7 Food-crop railings from stations in Southern Province. Sierra Leone, 1926-36
Source: Annual Report, Department of Agriculture, 1937.

the Sierra Leone Department of Agriculture, was 10 km to the north of Mano, and officials may have been right to conclude that to some extent the data on foodcrop railings reflected Njala influence. New planting materials introduced through Njala from 1912 onwards had helped diversify local food-crop agriculture. On the other hand, local resistance to swamp-rice cultivation suggests that farmers were very selective in their response to the Njala extension programme. This selectivity reflects the fact that local farmers had elaborated a set of interesting alternatives to the techniques for swamp rice conceived and recommended by the Agriculture Department. These local initiatives involved the combination of upland rice cultivation with two types of wet-land cultivation – cultivation of short-duration rices on run-off plots, and in areas of silty moisture-retentive soil, and cultivation of long-duration flood-tolerant rices, in valley bottoms and waterways. Although catenary farming systems of this sort are found throughout Sierra Leone (and indeed much of the rest of West Africa) their importance is especially great in this instance because of the geography of the region from Njala eastwards towards Bo.

The lowlands stretching back from the Sierra Leone coast are terminated by a pronounced escarpment running across the country from north-west to south-east (Figure 8). The scarp follows a geological boundary between the ancient sediments of the Rokel River Series and the predominantly granitic Pre-Cambrian Basement Complex. Much of the area at the foot of the scarp, underlain by the Rokel River Series, is covered by a series of infertile, seasonally-flooded, grassy depressions known as bolilands, some of which (in northern Sierra Leone) have been successfully developed for mechanized cultivation of swamp rices. By contrast, however, the southernmost portion of the area underlain by the Rokel River Series supports a more heavily forested vegetation, only occasionally interrupted by bolilands (Figure 9). The rivers in this area flow off the granite south-westwards and then turn to follow the line of the escarpment southwards. In consequence of a history of river capture and periodic shifts in meanders a complex series of river terraces has been built up at the foot of the escarpment. The scarp-foot zone from Yele to south of Bo and south-west to Njala and Mano thus constitutes a distinct geographical region, comprising a mosaic of infertile upland soils developed over the Rokel River Series, interrupted both by isolated boliland fragments and extensive facets of moisture-retentive and more fertile soils associated with the meandering of the major rivers at the foot of the scarp. I shall refer to this region, for convenience, as the scarp-foot zone of central Sierra Leone.

Techniques for exploiting these moist alluvial and colluvial soils are widespread and long-established throughout Sierra Leone and Liberia. They were noted, for example, by the Dutch traveller Olfert Dapper in the Cape Mount area in the seventeenth century (Jones, 1983: 165). What is unusual about the central Sierra Leone

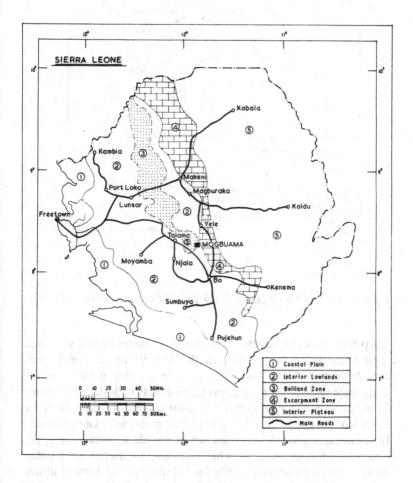

Figure 8   Scarp-foot zone in Sierra Leone. Map modified after Gwynne-Jones *et al.*

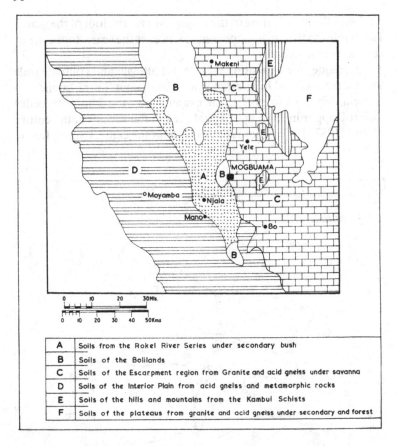

Figure 9 Soils in Mogbuama-Mano area. After van Vuure *et al.*, 1972.

scarp-foot zone, however, is the extent of farms of this sort, and their commercial importance in the last 50 years. Quick rices account for perhaps 10–20 per cent of all rice planted in the scarp-foot region, but for a disproportionately high share of income from rice sales, since the crop is ready for harvest at the height of the so-called 'hungry season' (August) when prices are at a maximum. In some cases special farms, known in Mende as **bulu** (sing.), are cleared for this purpose. In other cases quick varieties are planted on river-terrace materials at the foot of the 'upland' farm to utilize run-off therefrom.

Evidence of the long-established importance of sales of rice and other foodstuffs in even the more remote villages in the scarp-foot zone is not hard to find. Villages in the northern half of Kamajei Chiefdom, an area lacking in all-season road connections even today, were, until 1945, without access to vehicular transport for 15–20 km in any direction. Even so, older farmers recall regularly headloading rice down to the rail head at Mano or up to the gold mine at Baomahun in the Kangari Hills during the 1930s and 1940s. Many of the villages in the scarp-foot zone, especially those off the main roads (and in consequence less affected by the loss of labour by outmigration) continue to be noted for their rice surpluses, and for the availability of rice during the 'hungry season'. Much of this surplus is channelled to Bo, the major urban centre in the region. A number of villages in the northern part of the scarp-foot zone sell to rice dealers from the Kono diamond fields. Yele is the centre for this trade.

Some centres in the scarp-foot zone are especially well-known as focuses of indigenous agricultural experimentation. The town of Bumpe is frequently cited as the point of origin of many local cultivation techniques and rice varieties. Equally frequently it is the place to which farmers would refer if asked about older rice varieties not now generally cultivated. On the other hand, neither Bumpe, nor the scarp-foot zone more generally, has figured much in formal accounts of agricultural land-use and farming systems in Sierra Leone. A rare exception, in print, is an entry in Deighton's *Vernacular botanical vocabulary for Sierra Leone* (1957: 96) which defines **bulu** as 'a small field of early rice sown on low-lying ground' and adds that 'certain short-duration rice varieties are sown in such places before the main upland rice sowing, and [are] harvested in July–August: especially common in parts of Moyamba District, e.g. Bumpe'.

The suggestion, then, is that the scarp-foot zone of central Sierra Leone is characteristic of an important but neglected 'tier' in West African food-production economies, namely ecological regions which have responded effectively to market demands for increased output of food, but which are insufficiently large or important, by themselves, to have attracted the attention of the 'formal' research sector. In this respect the scarp-foot zone in Sierra Leone stands in marked contrast to the Scarcies estuaries, where rice cultivation in the mangrove swamps has been 'visible' to, and well-supported by, the 'formal' research sector since the 1930s. (The Rokupr research station was established specifically to support Scarcies rice cultivation, though its remit has since become much broader.) The scarp-foot zone is not, by itself, sufficiently important to rice production in Sierra Leone to warrant a specialist research station. But it is exactly for this reason that it would make a good setting in which to explore the possibilities of R & D programmes building on farmers' own discoveries. The first requirements in this respect are a better understanding of the way in which local farmers manage 'quick rice' cultivation on run-off plots (and moisture-retentive soils more generally), and some understanding of how this type of indigenous wet-land management technique is integrated with other farming activities.

Farming systems in two scarp-foot villages

Rice farms and soils

This account of scarp-foot rice farming systems in central Sierra Leone is based on detailed studies in Mogbuama, a relatively isolated village of c. 550 persons in Kamajei Chiefdom, and additional material from Bauya, a village of c. 250 persons, close to the former railway line, in Kowa Chiefdom. Kamajei and Kowa are chiefdoms with low population density (between 10 and 20 persons per km^2) and low rates of population increase. In common with many exclusively rural chiefdoms in Sierra Leone, natural increase in population over the past two or three decades tends to have been counterbalanced by rural out-migration. Mogbuama stands exactly on the junction between the Rokel River Series and the granitic Pre-Cambrian Basement Complex. West and south-west of Mogbuama there is an extensive zone of river terraces and levees. Nearly all the soils in this river-terrace zone are silty and moisture-retentive, and thus are suitable for the cultivation of quick rices on an extensive scale. Some farmers integrate a main farm on silty soil with a valley-bottom farm for swamp rices. Long-duration 'floating' rices are planted in inland valley swamps. The three main rivers flowing through Mogbuama territory are lined by flood-plain grassland, known in Mende as **bati**. Special techniques have been developed (see below) for cultivation of swamp rice in these grassland areas. East of Mogbuama, on the granites, and around Bauya, the landscape is more deeply dissected. In both environments farmers tend to make farms which combine all three elements in the catenary sequence. Medium duration 'upland' rices are planted on the gravelly soils of the upper slopes, quick rices are cultivated on the silty lower-slope soils, and long-duration swamp varieties in the valley bottoms.

Soils with a high silt content are classified by farmers as belonging to a group known in Mende as **tumu**. Soils in this group predominate in the river terrace zone west of Mogbuama. Upper slope soils in catenary sequences are either **koti** (rocky) or **ngoyo** (stony) depending on the character of the gravel fraction. East of Mogbuama the gravels are mixtures of granite and laterite. Around Bauya gravels are derived mainly from laterite (plinthite glaebules). Not all farmers distinguish rocky and stony soils, preferring instead to use the term **koti** to cover any free-draining gravelly upland soil. Lower slope soils in catenary sequences are **tumu** (silty), **nganya** (sandy), or mixtures, e.g. **koti-ndumu** ('t' mutates to 'nd' in Kpa-Mende). The term **pete-pete** (cf. Krio/ Yoruba **potopoto** = muddy, swampy) is used to refer to valley-bottom, hydromorphic, soils. The swamps themselves are further subdivided according to whether they are seasonally flooded grasslands (**bati**), 'shallow' (wet-season) swamps (**kpete**), or 'deep' (permanently waterlogged) swamps (**yenge gbete**).

The differences of soil type recognized by farmers are readily apparent in data stemming from laboratory analysis of Mogbuama soil samples. Sediment analysis picks out the differences between the three main elements in the soil catena: swamp, lower slope and upper slope soils (Figure 10). An analysis of organic matter content again clearly differentiates swamp, river terrace and upland soils (Figure 11). In this case, however, it is perhaps surprising to note that **koti** and **ngoyo** soils appear to have a higher organic matter content than **tumu** and **nganya** soils. This may reflect the fact that it is the custom to allow vegetation in the granite zone to the east of the village to fallow for longer than vegetation in the river terrace zone to the west (c. 10–20 years as opposed to 8–11 years: Figure 12). The swamp forest vegetation in the river-terrace zone is reckoned to be impenetrably difficult to clear if left for too long.

Rice planting strategies
Quick rices are planted, from April onwards, on **tumu** and **nganya** soils, and sometimes also in **bati** farms, and harvested after 90–120 days (mid-July to mid-September). Medium duration 'upland' rices are planted on free-draining **koti** soils during June and July, and

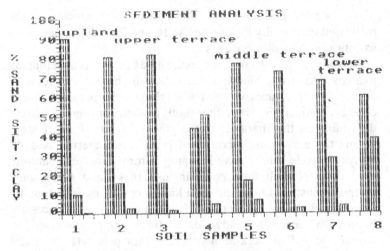

Figure 10   Sediment analysis of main types of soil catena

harvested after 120–140 days (in October and November). Long-duration 'floating' rices are planted in valley swamps and water courses in July–August and harvested after 140–160 days (late November to early January).

Quick rices are generally reckoned to be less reliable than the medium-duration varieties. This is partly in the nature of the varieties themselves. Speed of ripening is sometimes correlated with lightness of yield. In addition, early rices are subject to especially intense attack by birds, because they have few alternative sources of food during the period that quick rices are ripening. Farmers are partly compensated for these risks by the greater fertility of many silty, river-terrace soils in the scarp zone, when compared to gravelly upland soils (van Vuure, Odell & Sutton, 1972).

Most farmers aim to combine cultivation of all three types of rice – quick, medium and long duration – in order to balance their risks and to smooth out the labour profile. In Mogbuama, typical figures for plantings per household are 15–20 per cent quick varieties, 65–70 per cent medium-duration varieties, and 15 per cent long-duration varieties. On 'catenary' farms east of the village, the

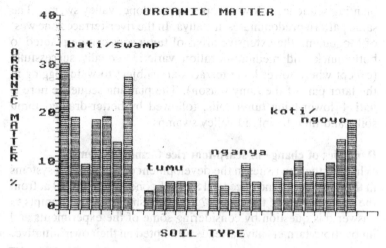

Figure 11 Organic matter analysis of three soil types

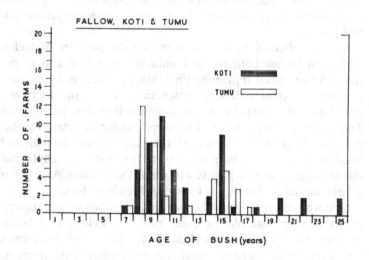

Figure 12 Fallow periods on Mogbuama farms

planting sequence is lower slope, upper slope, valley swamp. The same pattern predominates in Bauya. In the river-terrace zone west of Mogbuama the extensive areas of **tumu** soils can be planted to both quick and medium-duration varieties equally successfully (except where lower-lying terraces are subject to waterlogging in the later part of the rainy season). The planting sequence here is **bati** + lower-lying **tumu** soils, followed by better-drained **tumu** soils, and then by inland valley swamps.

Dynamics of change in scarp-foot rice farming systems
What are the key issues in the development of rice farming systems in the scarp-foot zone of central Sierra Leone, when looked at from the point of view of the farmer? The assessment below attempts to answer this question by considering some of the experiments and innovations farmers have already attempted on their own initiative.

Innovations in labour organization
A major problem with quick rices is that they are subject to greater than average climatic uncertainty, leading in turn to acute labour supply difficulties. Provided the soil is adequately moisture-retentive and the crop well-sited in relation to run-off the danger of drought damage is relatively slight. There is a much greater danger, however, from an *excess* of early rainfall. Early rainfall may severely inhibit the burning of cleared vegetation. Weed growth is especially rapid on badly burnt farms, and is a major impediment to. rice planting.

Farmers affected by a poor burn face the problem of finding additional labour both to clear unburnt vegetation and to hoe through extra weed at planting time. Since planting is, in any case, the most intractable of labour bottlenecks on the upland rice farm, a poor burn may convert a difficult situation into an untenable one. Those with extensive areas of low-lying, moisture-retentive, soils may find themselves, in a year of unseasonally early rainfall, with large sections of their farm incomplete (uncleared, or unplanted) due to difficulty in securing extra labour at short notice. A section of a farm wasted in this way is known in Mende as **lobai**.

One way of coping with the especially onerous labour requirements of a sizeable plot of quick rice is to belong to a labour co-operative. In Mogbuama about 20 per cent of all agricultural labour is provided by labour co-operatives. These co-operatives – of which there are six distinct types involving the majority of the village's agriculturally active male population (but a much smaller percentage of the female population) – are especially prominent during rice planting and harvest; periods of acute labour supply difficulty.

The right moment to burn, plant and harvest varies from farm to farm. When that moment comes the work needs to be completed as swiftly and effectively as possible. Part of the appeal of labour co-operatives is that they apply timely labour in a concentrated and disciplined manner. Another factor of importance is that membership of a reciprocal co-operative is an effective guarantee that labour will be available when needed. This is important in communities experiencing general labour shortages, where even farmers with cash to hire labour commonly find that 'contracted' labour fails to turn out on the day expected (having being diverted by a rival's better 'bid').

Innovations in labour organization are important features of agricultural change in both Bauya and Mogbuama. In some cases 'traditional' forms of 'communal' labour organization have been adapted to modern circumstances. A co-operative may start off, for example, by being modelled on the reciprocal work groups formed by young men to perform 'bride service' for their prospective fathers-in-law. One labour co-operative in Mogbuama is called **mbla** ('father-in-law') for this reason. But the members are now working for themselves, and their working practices, and procedures for settling disputes, are entirely 'modern'. These include a written constitution, regular business meetings, and clock-regulated time keeping. In other cases, ideas about labour organization have been imported from other parts of the country. The Temne are especially admired for the way in which they are able to form and train up teams of very young farm workers capable of great feats of labour endurance. These groups operate with almost military discipline and precision. Each has its 'regimental' flag and band, and harsh and humiliating punishments for slackness (e.g. inability to keep up with the general work rate of the group). Much of the work is done on an aggressively competitive basis. Farmers in the Mogbuama area form young people into a type of group they call **gboto** apparently in direct imitation of **kabotho** groups among the Temne.

Innovations in planting material and planting practices
Rice farmers in the scarp-foot zone deploy a large range of planting

materials and are constantly on the look out for more. In Mogbuama alone, in 1983, 98 farm households planted a total of 59 distinct rice varieties – 18 of which were quick rices, 31 medium-duration upland rices and the balance long-duration swamp varieties. Each farm household would, on average, make use of 4–8 varieties: 2–3 quick rices, 3–4 upland rices, and 1–2 swamp rices. Changes are frequent. A sample of 30 households reported 73 cases of new or unfamiliar varieties adopted in the last 10 years or so. Some changes were forced by circumstances (where a farmer shifted from **tumu** to **koti** soils, or where poor results dictated the need for a change), but in others (perhaps as many as a third of all instances cited) the main factor appears to have been experimental curiosity – a desire to try out unfamiliar material or to see what a familiar variety might do under unusual conditions.

New planting material is mostly begged or bought from friends, strangers and visitors, or acquired in the course of travels to other parts of the country. Some rices are adventitious arrivals. The name of one Mogbuama rice variety – **tokpoeihu** – denotes that it was first found germinated on the crown of a palm tree, where local opinion reckons it must have been dropped by a passing bird. Other rices are the result of natural crossing, or the outworking of specific characteristics in genetically variable planting material.

Rice harvesting in the scarp-foot zone (as in much of Mende land) is done with a knife, panicle by panicle. Although this is more labour-intensive than sickle harvesting it allows for the careful roguing of off-types during the harvest. Rogued material is frequently kept for experiment. For convenience, the first trials tend to be carried out near the farm hut. Full-scale trials are typically undertaken in the seep-zone, from which point the farmer has the option of moving further up slope or down into the swamp proper. In some instances the plot will be carefully marked, and note taken of input–output ratios (the same vessel – a calabash or tin – will be used to measure the amounts of seed planted and harvested). Any new or unfamiliar planting material, however acquired, is liable to be tested in this way. In Mende, farm experiments of this sort are termed **hugo** or **saini**. It seems probable that an experimental approach is a long-established and widespread element in Mende agriculture, and in farming communities throughout Sierra Leone (the point is discussed further in Chapter 6).

None of the rices currently grown in Mogbuama or Bauya is a

directly-introduced 'improved' variety. Some of the swamp rices appear to trace back ultimately to introductions by the colonial Department of Agriculture (e.g. a variety known as **pladisi**, from Temne **padisi**, ex Demerara Creole, introduced *c.* 1914 from British Guiana). Many – perhaps the majority – of the best quick and medium-duration varieties are local selections. The most reliable, and one of the most widely planted, medium-duration rices – gbengben – is said to have been developed from an older indigenous variety, **nduliwa**, by farmers in the Bumpe area, *c.* 40–50 years ago. A man who claims to have been among the first to plant **gbengben** in Mogbuama recalls first seeing it in Mano in 1935, later acquiring half a bushel as a gift from his mother-in-law.

In fieldwork in Mogbuama in 1983, I came across three or four cases where farmers were currently undertaking trials involving selections derived from material rogued from earlier harvests. Perhaps the most interesting of these cases involved a popular, high-yielding, quick rice, known as **jewule**, first introduced to Mogbuama from the Njala area *c.* 10–15 years ago. The farmer concerned had selected a variant on **jewule** that had begun to develop long awns. Mende farmers are often interested in awned varieties (Plate 4), and in varieties which possess long outer glumes (**kalembamei**, lit. 'jaw-boned rice'). Whereas textbooks tend to advise selection to *eliminate* these characteristics, the Mende farmer has the view that both properties are useful in deterring birds. Since bird damage is a major difficulty for the cultivator of quick rices, the idea of an awned variant of **jewule** is one to attract considerable local attention.

Variation on the intercropping theme was another issue to attract considerable attention among local experimenters in Mogbuama and Bauya. In Bauya, an area better suited to tree-crop cultivation than Mogbuama, a number of farmers have experimented with ways of cropping infant palm-oil plantations on **tumu** soils with rice and cow peas. The site is brushed and planted with rice, and then, after the rice harvest, with cowpeas, while being concurrently interplanted with palm seedlings. One farmer, having thus established a plantation of widely-spaced and well-pruned palms, has since experimented to see if there is sufficient sunlight in the early part of the year to allow regular cultivation of quick rice under mature palms.

In Mogbuama, some farmers have shown a particular interest in innovative uses of **bati** lands. The idea of intercropping a **bati** with a

Plate 4 Awned rice

quick rice and a long-duration floating rice is to harvest the quick rice before the **bati** is completely drowned by the riverine flood in the later part of the rainy season, leaving behind a densely-tillering swamp rice sufficiently well-established to cope with the deep water on the **bati** in August and September (Figure 13). Thus the **bati** is first harvested in June/July and then again in September/October when the flood finally recedes. In one case examined in 1983, the quick rice gave a yield of about 2400 kg/ha, and the second crop about 600 kg/ha. The farmer concerned planned the further experiment of attempting to grow a final crop of maize between October and December to utilize residual moisture.

Although the basic idea of intercropping quick and long-duration rices on **bati** land has been well-known for a generation or more, those making such farms show much experimental interest in finding the right mix of varieties and the right proportions in which to combine them. A quick variety that proves a shade too slow may be caught by the flood. A long-duration variety that tillers too profusely too early may compete with and thus depress yields of the quick variety.

Farmer experiments in swamp cultivation
Rice cultivation in inland valley swamps – the key to increased rice output in Sierra Leone, according to the majority of development plans and agencies – is practised quite widely in both Mogbuama and Bauya, but only rarely with any attempt at water-control. Mogbuama farmers are less enthusiastic about swamp cultivation than farmers in Bauya.

Mogbuama farmers are aware that swamp soils are especially fertile, and that swamp rice yields are often very high. The main reason they give for not pursuing this option more enthusiastically is that the rices involved are mainly long-duration varieties ready for harvest late in the year when rice supplies are abundant and prices low. Unlike quick rices, they offer neither a solution to the problem of the hungry season, nor the prospect of sales at tip-top prices. In addition, swamp rices are considered, by local standards, to taste very poor. They are suitable only for sale, not for consumption.

Swamp rice cultivation, therefore, is seen in Mogbuama as a useful adjunct to other types of rice cultivation, but few farmers are prepared to accord it much priority. This explains the local preference for flood-tolerant varieties, and minimalist cultivation strategies. Planting a swamp and allowing it to fend for itself, more or less, is how members of the farm household convert to profitable use any time left over after solving more pressing problems on the main farm.

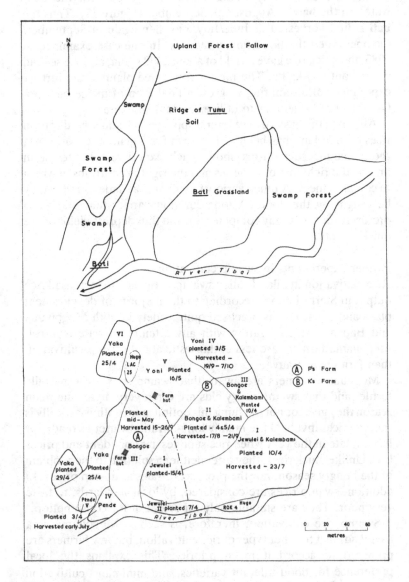

Figure 13 **Bati** farm in Mogbuama

In Bauya, the picture is rather different. Here, tree crops are given greater emphasis. Conditions are quite suitable for both oil palms and coffee (only coffee is successful in Mogbuama). In recent decades Bauya farmers have been steadily developing small tree-crop plantations on uplands and areas of river-terrace soils, and are now interested in swamp rice cultivation as a means to replace rice previously grown on upland farms. The majority of farmers still prefer a system integrating quick and medium-duration rices on valley slopes with some swamp cultivation at the foot of the slope. To expand emphasis on swamp farming without eating into labour required for the upland farm, some farmers have turned to hiring tractors (from Njala) to cultivate swamps. Others have begun to substitute water-controlled swamp cultivation for upland farming.

A farm of this latter type (in a village adjacent to Bauya) is illustrated in Figure 14. It is worth noting that although at first glance this farm fits rather closely the general 'model' for small-

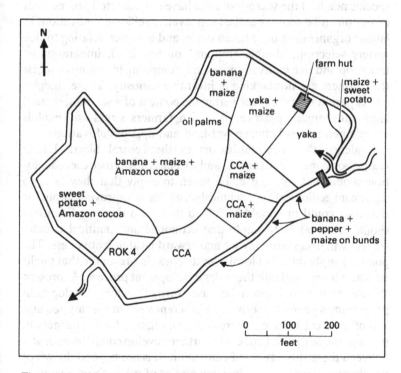

Figure 14 Water-controlled swamp, Bauya

farmer rice production systems advocated by many of the development agencies, it is, on closer inspection, a distinctly idiosyncratic creation. Bunding allows for water-control, but the farmer has deliberately chosen not to level the bunded area, preferring instead to engineer a slight gradient in order to recreate some of the features and opportunities of a run-off farm. The resulting diversity of soil moisture regimes allows the farmer to plant a range of rice varieties – some quick, some medium, and some of long-duration – both to spread the workload and to ensure a harvest season lasting over the greater part of the year. Some areas of the farm are double cropped. A further departure from the 'standard' swamp model is that the farmer has introduced an intercropping system in which rice and a variety of vegetable crops are grown alongside cocoa and bananas (Plate 5).

The lessons of the case-study

Low population densities and lack of research directed to the specific needs of the scarp-foot zone have not inhibited processes of invention and discovery at the local level. Significant innovations in labour organization have taken place, and evidence relating to rice variety selection, 'double cropping' on **bati** land, integration of tree-crop and rice cultivation, and intercropping in swamps suggest that farmers are not lacking in inventive curiosity. These changes and experiments take place within the context of a set of integrated land-management practices in which farmers stress and exploit complementarities between wet-land and upland cultivation.

Evidence that rice cultivators in the central Sierra Leone scarp-foot zone are inventive and oriented towards experimentation should not, of course, be taken to imply that they face no significant ecological and technical obstacles to improved output, or that they could or should be left to their own devices. Even less should it be taken to imply that economic and political circumstances will necessarily favour and reward local inventiveness. The point is simply this: that local inventiveness is a resource that might be better integrated into the wider development process. At present this tends not to happen because 'formal sector' development programmes promote swamp rice as a *replacement* for rain-fed and run-off rice cultivation, whereas the emphasis of most farmers in much of the scarp-foot zone is to further develop *complementarities* between these three types of cultivation. It is not beyond the wit of development agencies or the competence of research programmes

Plate 5 Indigenous water-controlled swamp at Bauya

to collaborate with farmers in the further development of appropriately integrated rice farming systems.

Food-crop farming in western Nigeria

The second case-study looks at food-crop farming in the forest zone of western Nigeria. The area concerned, a belt of 'oil-palm bush' between Lagos lagoon and the Niger Delta, is farmed by a Yoruba-speaking group known as the Ikale (Figure 15a). Population densities are five to ten times higher than in the scarp-foot zone of central Sierra Leone. The lessons to be drawn from evidence of dynamism and inventiveness in Ikale food-crop production are similar to those deriving from the Sierra Leonian study. In discussing the Ikale case, however, more attention is paid to social and political factors which have helped render many of these changes invisible to planners and policy makers.

The ecology of Ikale agriculture
The red sandy-loam soils of Ikale country derive from unconsolidated Tertiary sands. They are free-draining, moderately fertile but

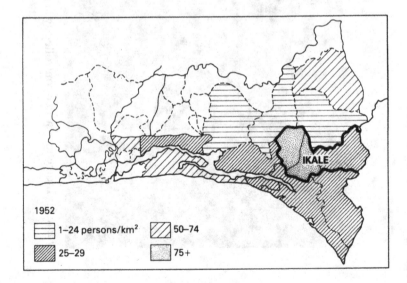

Figure 15a   Ikale: location and population densities

easily eroded. Rainfall is over 2000 mm per year, and the rainy season is lengthy (9–10 months). The south-eastern tip of Ikale country adjoining the Niger Delta is transitional from tropical (seasonal) to equatorial (year-round) rainfall. In terms of soil and climate the area has more in common with the 'palm belt' of middle-western and central-eastern Nigeria than with the cocoa belt to the north, where rainfall is less and the dry season longer, but where soils developed over Basement Complex granites are more fertile and moisture-retentive (Figure 15b).

In agricultural terms, Ikale country is well-suited to cultivation of root crops (yams, cassava and cocoa yams) and to the oil palm, which grows profusely in forest regrowth. Rotational fallowing by food-crop farmers over the last 100 years has converted secondary forest to 'oil palm bush'. For much of the twentieth century Ikale has been among the more important palm-oil producing districts west of the Niger. For the most part, Ikale landlords preferred to rent their palm groves to Urhobo migrants from the Delta. The Urhobo are noted specialists in harvesting wild palms and producing oil. Ikale landlords collected rents from the Urhobo, and concentrated on producing food surpluses which they then sold to the Urhobo.

More recently, some Ikale farmers have attempted to diversify their activities by planting tree crops, notably cocoa, coffee and kola. Cocoa, potentially the most profitable of these tree crops, rarely succeeds in local soils. Ikale farmers find more suitable moisture-retentive soils for cocoa where the Tertiary Sands give way to the granites along the border with Ondo District. Ondo and Ikale migrant farmers have contested land in this border zone for 60 years or more (Adejuyigbe, 1975). Within the last 15 years several large palm-oil plantations have been established in Ikale country to feed a major palm mill in Okitipupa, the district headquarters. Small-holders have been encouraged to develop their own palm plantations and affiliate to the scheme as 'out-growers'. Urhobo migrants have increasingly abandoned the hard life of harvesting wild palms, and have moved into trade of various forms, and into food-stuff processing, especially the manufacture of cassava meal (Otite, 1979).

Experiment and innovation in Ikale agriculture

When Ikale farming systems are examined in detail, evidence of experimental, adaptive, innovative action by small-holders is as

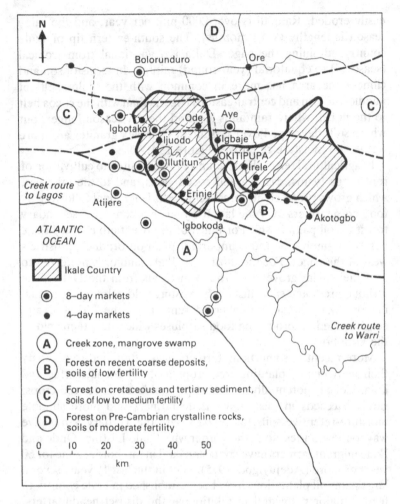

Figure 15b Ikale: ecological/vegetation/geological zones and main markets and trade routes

abundant as in the Sierra Leonian case. Two changes stand out among the major innovations:

1   The emergence of the Ikale–Urhobo partnership as a way of exploiting the extensive areas of palm-oil bush.
2   Diversification of root-crop production through the wide-spread adoption of cassava.

Fieldwork in the early 1970s (Richards, 1977) revealed much experimentation at farm level. Many farmers – worried by reduced fallows and declining fertility on root-crop farms – had either experimented with new intercrop mixes (e.g. increasing the ratio of water yam [*Dioscorea alata*] to white yam [*Dioscorea rotundata*]) or were actively developing 'compound' farms, fertilized by household refuse. It was common to see some of the biggest and best white yams grown around the farm house in 'inverted heaps' (hollows scooped out and filled with compost).

Two particular instances are indicative of the local scope for 'populist' strategies of agricultural change.

Ikale farmers are noted experts in yam cultivation but now they grow more cassava than yam. Cassava is more 'labour efficient' and less demanding of soil fertility than white yam. These adjustments to changed ecological conditions, labour-supply constraints and new market opportunities, have not been undertaken without a sense of regret. Some farmers continue to experiment with yam, partly for the hell of it, partly because it is still a 'preferred' crop.

Some years ago the International Institute of Tropical Agriculture in Ibadan (IITA) decided to work on the problem of germinating yams from true seed. So-called 'seed yams' are either tubers grown especially for planting, or setts (portions of full-grown tubers set aside for planting purposes). Either way, between a quarter and one-third of the edible portion of the crop has to be set aside for replanting purposes. If yams could be grown from true seed then yields would be increased by the proportion of the harvest of tubers normally set aside for planting purposes.

Ways of breaking seed dormancy were discovered, and there was every prospect of raising future crops in this way. Unfortunately, it was then discovered that the practical application of this discovery tends to be limited by the fact that the 'first generation' tubers are very small. Nor were IITA researchers the first to make these discoveries. A number of groups throughout the yam-growing belt of southern and central Nigeria were already familiar with the idea of raising yams from true seed. One Ikale farmer I knew claimed to have first explored such possibilities in the 1930s. When asked why he pursued the technique after discovering that the results were not very exciting, he told me, with some exasperation at having to put the obvious into words, that he did it 'for experiment'.

This story neatly underlines the point that West African small-holders are no strangers to the idea of agricultural experimentation, and that interest is sometimes the only reward asked. But of course, not all farmers' discoveries are so disappointing in practical outcome. A second case, with results of considerable economic significance, concerns the Variegated Grasshopper (*Zonocerus variegatus* L.), a cassava pest of epidemic proportions in Ikale country in the late 1960s and early 1970s. Research had indicated that the simplest and most effective approach to the control of this pest might be to mark out egg-laying sites in the late dry season and to dig them up later in the year. Typically, there would be only one or two such sites per hectare, so the task could be readily accomplished by each farmer for his or her own farm.

A key to such a control strategy would be whether or not farmers recognized the significance of such sites. In the event, Ikale farmers proved to have a wealth of careful observations concerning the insect's behaviour, including a knowledge of likely egg-laying sites, e.g. around old tree stumps, under piles of cleared vegetation, in damper soils generally (Page & Richards, 1977). This was demonstrated to me in striking fashion when, in 1976, a year when Variegated Grasshopper populations were low, a group of farmers from Iju Odo were able to locate all egg-laying sites active on their farm land that year, and later were able to take me straight to examples up to 3–4 km distant from the town.

In Chapter 6 I shall discuss the significance of detailed ecological knowledge of this kind for 'populist' approaches to pest control. For the moment, however, the question I want to raise is why development agencies are not more attuned to the innovative, experimental, adaptive skills of typical small-scale producers in African agriculture. Since the pioneering work of Polly Hill (1963) demonstrated the overwhelming importance of indigenous initiative in establishing cocoa cultivation in Ghana, commentators have been more circumspect in applying the 'conservative peasant' label to West African 'export crop' producers. Where cultivators specialize in food crops, however, blanket generalizations of the following kind tend to colour the perceptions of outside agencies:

In African countries...methods of production are still largely pre-scientific...What the peasant needs to know is not systematised into a set of absolute hypotheses ready to be tested...there is little understanding and tolerance of experimentation and limited scope for problem-solving... (Hyden, 1983: 5)

It will be clear from the material so far presented in this chapter that judgements of this sort are wide of the mark. But why are they so often made? The answer, I will suggest, is that food producing communities have frequently misled outsiders into thinking that not much was going on. It is often to the advantage of food producers to keep a 'low profile', politically speaking. The image of a 'subsistence backwater' is as good as any to fend off the tax gatherer and others interested in taking a share of what is often a thriving trade in basic foodstuffs. The trouble is that this tactic sometimes rebounds with unforseen consequences. The Ikale seem to have been so successful at disguising their participation in the wider regional economy that the chapter on cassava production in the National Accelerated Food Production Plan (NAFPP, 1977) missed them out entirely, despite their long-established importance in supplying cassava to much of the creek and lagoon region and western Delta (Figure 16).

Ikale in the regional foodstuffs economy

The creek and lagoon waterway system on the southern margin of Ikale country has been a major inter-regional trade route for many centuries, linking places as far apart as Whydah and trading centres in the Niger Delta. When agents of the Church Missionary Society first crossed Ikale *en route* to Ondo in the 1870s Ikale farmers were already involved in regional foodstuffs trade to the creek zone and to some of the trading centres in the western Delta, in return for fish, salt and imported cloth. Much of this trade was directed through Atijere and other important markets along the main creek routeway (Fig. 15b).

The Ikale were distinguished from other groups in the area south of Ondo by the extent to which they concentrated on food-crop agriculture, in preference to direct involvement in the overseas export trade. The Ikale had a number of settlements – **ode** – through which they dealt with the outside world, but for the most part they were resident in dispersed farm estates.

In 1872, Roger Goldsworthy, an agent of the Lagos government, found it difficult to settle a trade dispute between the Igbobini and the Ikale people of Irele because the latter 'were all absent at their farms' (Goldsworthy, 1872). The missionary Maser (1874), visiting Oke (Ode?) Aye in 1873, noted that the 'very good houses' belonging to the Ikale were 'generally quite empty and only occupied on special occasions' because the people 'live in thick bush on agriculture and change their abode after the land has been

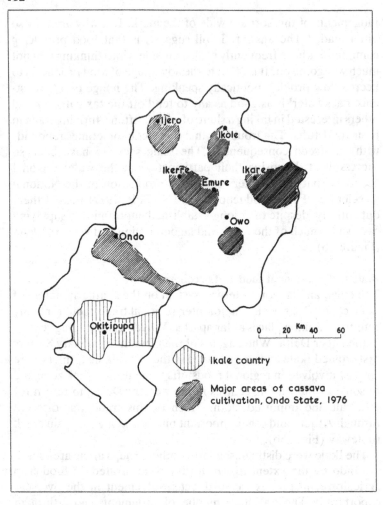

Figure 16 NAFPP cassava areas
Source: NAFPP (1977).

exhausted'. A quarter of a century later, Travelling Commissioner Ambrose attempted to persuade the people of Irele, 'scattered among their farms', to rebuild Ode Irele. They did so, but 'straightway left it again' (Ambrose, 1900).

During the early years of colonial rule Ikale was the scene of a significant factional struggle between the Ijamo, a chieftancy society representing the interests of the heads of food-producing farm estates, and a group supporting Nigwo, chief of Igbotako. Nigwo was a Christian convert, sympathetic to the interests of the export trade (at that time predominantly concerned with wild rubber and timber) and recognized by the British as the local paramount. Nigwo was seen by the British as an 'enlightened' ruler, and the Ijamo as died-in-the-wool traditionalists. In 1908 the British mounted a 'show of force' against Nigwo's opponents on the grounds of their support for barbaric practices such as ritual twin murder.

The Ijamo were 'guardians of the land' and were much exercised by issues of sexual morality. There is some possibility that they thought twinning evidence of adultery, and considered this a threat to their farm labour, already depleted by the defection of young people, clients and servile labour to centres connected with the export trade. If this interpretation is correct, then the Ijamo were not especially 'traditional' or 'backward', but were concerned to defend their well-developed foodstuff trading interests against damage caused by the rapid growth of the overseas export sector.

The victory of Nigwo's 'overseas trade' faction backed by British colonial force required the 'food' party in Ikale politics to modify its tactics. In the immediate aftermath of the 1908 'show of strength' it was noted, in the Annual Report for Southern Nigeria, 1908, that 'buyers of palm produce...had increased seven-fold'. By the 1920s Okitipupa Division exported annually about 5000 tons of palm oil (about 10 per cent of all palm-oil exports from western Nigeria), the bulk of this oil coming from the Ikale districts.

The rapid development of the palm trade depended on two circumstances:

1   Ikale success in building up population and converting large areas of once thick forest to palm-oil bush through vigorous food crop cultivation (many other areas of west and west-central Africa, afflicted by the rush for rubber, timber and ivory, *lost* population during the same period: cf. Suret-Canale, 1971).

2   An influx of palm-harvesting specialists from the Urhobo districts of the Niger Delta. This was partly a consequence of British political intervention on the Benin River and disruption of the established trading relations between the Urhobo and Itsekiri (Ikime, 1969).

During the 1920s British administrators frequently gave vent to their surprise that the Ikale were prepared to rent their palm groves to the migrant Urhobo rather than harvesting the palms for themselves. The view of the administration was that the area was very much a backwater, only slowly emerging into the modern world, and that local land-owners had not yet woken up to the value of participation in the palm-oil trade. But in fact, what Ikale land-owners had found out was that they could make money both from renting their palm groves to the Urhobo and from selling food to them.

Table 6 compares estimated annual *per capita* income for a yam farmer and palm collector in Ikale for four years, 1928, 1932, 1965 and 1971 (the first two figures are for years either side of the collapse in export prices in 1929, and the second pair for years immediately prior and subsequent to the Nigerian civil war). Income from oil palm was superior to food-crop production only in the last of these years, and then only if oil had been sold in local markets and not at prices offered by the government marketing board. The superiority of oil palm in 1971 (as a result of a buoyant post-war domestic market) correlates with Ikale land-owners beginning for the first time to show an interest in exploiting their own palms and in establishing small plantations.

The depression years of the 1930s, in particular, underlined the economic rationality of the food production alternative, since food prices dropped less than prices for palm products. Whereas many of the Urhobo had to return home, their landlords being unwilling to rent them land for food production, Ikale food-crop farmers still kept open the options of selling food to the Urhobo remaining and

Table 6 *Income from yam farming and palm harvesting in Ikale*

	Ikale yam farmer	Urhobo palm collector	
1928	₦ 105	₦ 81	
1932	₦ 110	₦ 23	
1965	₦ 190	₦ 141[†]	₦ 185*
1971	₦ 285	₦ 156[†]	₦ 324*

[†] Sales to Marketing Board for export.   ₦ 1.00 = £1.17 (1971)
* Sales of palm oil in local markets.

Source: Richards (1977: 251).

of continuing to participate in regional exchanges of food for fish with the creek-side communities to the south. If all else failed, they could look forward to secure subsistence at a time when urban wage workers and producers committed to the export trade faced prospects of severe privation.

It would seem to be no accident that the 1930s were years of resurgence for the 'food party' in Ikale politics. Ikale chiefs petitioned to allow the reconstitution of the Ijamo Society in 1931. This request bore fruit in the Intelligence Report of 1937, which proposed making the reconstituted Ijamo Society a cornerstone of a reformed system of Indirect Rule. Trade recession had brought home the point that food producers may make unexciting profits but that they survive in good order in difficult times.

'Subsistence' misunderstood?
There is a tendency in the literature on West African agriculture to assume that concentration on food production signifies a 'subsistence' orientation, lack of 'penetration' by market forces, or the 'survival' of elements of a pre-capitalist 'mode of production'. Murray Last (1980) has suggested that this is to confuse history and geography. His argument is that groups such as the 'pagan' Maguzawa of Hausaland are distinctive not because they are isolated 'survivals' from an earlier epoch, but because they specialize in low-profit/low-risk activities like food production and local trade rather than in high-profit/high-risk activities linked to urban merchants and long-distance trade routes. Food production is unspectacular. Serious food producers often prefer to live 'on the farm' in 'deep rural' locations. Frequently, as Maser and Goldsworthy found with the Ikale in the 1870s, food producers tend not to be around when visitors call. Urban-based planners and policy makers are too often tied to their vehicles and the roadside (Chambers, 1983). They tend not to follow where the food production action is, so to speak, with the result that in normal times food production slips below the threshold of official perception. This 'invisibility' of food-crop producers is compounded by male bias (Rogers, 1980). In a number of cases key innovations in the West African food-crop sector have been undertaken by women farmers (Dey, 1981; Guyer, 1980). Among the Ngwa of eastern Nigeria, for example, there was wide-spread adoption of cassava as a food crop by women farmers during the period 1917 to 1928, a change with important implications for the continued expansion of palm oil production for

export (Martin, 1984). Academic and professional commentators on African agriculture have too often tended either to ignore female farming or to assume that it was undertaken entirely for subsistence purposes.

Bad times tend to sharpen the focus, however. When urban food shortages become a major political issue planning survey teams may reach to the remotest villages. But, as one Mende farmer told Michael Johnny, 'if the farmer runs heedlessly through the rice field just before harvest then the watchers know he is chasing something or something is chasing him', adding that villagers draw the same conclusion when city folk come around to ask after the farm (Johnny, 1979). In bad times – times of recession, great inflation or severe economic mismanagement – food producers, suspicious of earlier neglect, may react by withdrawing into subsistence, preferring to eat and drink rather than be forced to sell their surpluses at 'fixed' prices 'in the national interest'. This serves further to confirm the visitor's misconception that food producers are sunk in 'tradition' and 'backwardness' (and sometimes in 'drunkenness'). And so the cycle of misperception and misunderstanding repeats itself, with modern agricultural development projects no more able to extend relevant inputs to serious food producers in 'deep rural' settings than the British were able to comprehend and assist Ikale root-crop farmers in the 1920s.

Conclusion

The conclusion to these two case-studies is simple to state. West African food-crop producers are inventive, but development agencies rarely harness this inventiveness because they misunderstand the nature of both the agriculture and the politics of communities where food production is a major interest. The consequences of these misunderstandings continue to permeate research and development directed at the small-holder farming sector. The next two chapters outline some of these consequences and discuss ways of dealing with them.

5 Science and the peasantry

Introduction

Is science the key to an agricultural revolution in Africa? Many people think so. But on what evidence? Do they have specific historical precedents in mind? The changes in English agriculture grouped by historians under the heading 'the agricultural revolution' were brought about by farmers not scientists. If anything, the agricultural revolution stimulated the development of agricultural science, not the other way round.

My purpose in raising this point is not to argue that scientific research has no relevance to the development of West African agriculture – this would be an absurd conclusion – but to underline the point that the benefits are far from guaranteed. Much depends on the context within which the research system operates. In Western Europe or North America the farming community is highly-organized, politically influential, and better able to inject a sense of reality into otherwise 'impractical' research programmes, or to insist that serious attention be paid to its own agenda of research priorities. In West Africa, by contrast, a fragmented and relatively uninfluential small-holder farming community has few if any opportunities to state its research needs directly or formulate lists of priorities.

A key issue (illustrated by case-study material in this chapter) is that when 'applied', 'practically relevant', agricultural research is mooted in West Africa its 'relevance' has often been arrived at by dead reckoning – through conclusions scientists draw from their own theoretical models of what ought to be relevant – and not by involving farmers directly in the process of problem formulation. 'Relevance' on paper is not the same thing as relevance in practice. As a result some of the most impeccably 'practical' pieces of research end up with disappointingly few takers. Meanwhile the majority of West African farmers continue to rely on their own systems of knowledge and research procedures – systems and procedures of which scientists in the 'formal' sector are often quite unaware. At best the two systems pass like ships in the night. At worst they duplicate effort, or compete destructively.

Possible new bases for collaboration are considered in Chapter 6. The present chapter concentrates on a diagnosis of the problem. It does this by looking at two case-studies of attempts to foster African agricultural revolutions. An open verdict is returned on recent attempts to translate the Green Revolution into West African terms. This initiative has a number of promising features, but some obvious problems. The nature of these problems is thrown into greater relief by the second case-study, which concentrates on the lessons to be learnt from colonial attempts to rid Africa of the tsetse fly hazard, the key, so it was supposed, to an agricultural revolution based on 'mixed farming'. The chapter concludes by noting the way in which models of 'cultural evolution' have influenced research priorities in the absence of effective 'customer–contractor' relations in agricultural research directed towards the needs of small-scale farmers in West Africa.

A Green Revolution in West Africa?

The CG System

Until about 1965 agricultural research in West Africa, as in many other parts of the tropics, was heavily biased towards 'export' crops. Since then, much more attention has been paid to food crops. Much of this recent work on tropical food crops has been carried out under the auspices of an international research network co-ordinated by the Consultative Group on International Agricultural Research (CGIAR).

The CG System (as it may be conveniently termed) has been developed, largely with grants from the Ford and Rockefeller Foundations, and 'aid' money from the World Bank and the 'western' industrial nations, as a means to extend the benefits of the so-called Green Revolution as widely as possible within the tropics and sub-tropics (Table 7). It comprises ten International Agricultural Research Centres (IARCs) and a number of other research consortia and networks. Food-crop and livestock research are the exclusive concerns. The approach is primarily biological and technological, though some attention is paid to economic and social factors insofar as these are relevant to the implementation of biological or technological innovations.

The Green Revolution is a phrase coined in the 1960s to describe the increased output obtainable from improved wheat and rice varieties developed by plant breeding research programmes in Mexico and the Philippines. Norman Borlaug, working in Mexico in the 1950s, produced a series of dwarf wheat varieties which were unaffected by varying day lengths, adapted to a wide range of environments, and high-yielding when adequately watered and fertilized. The outstanding success of these wheats prompted workers at the International Rice Research Institute (IRRI) in the Philippines to follow a similar path in developing improved rices.

An early example of an IRRI high-yielding variety (HYV) is the rice known as IR8 (first released in 1966). IR8 was developed by crossing a dwarf early-maturing Japonica rice from Taiwan with a tall Indonesian variety. The result was a short-straw, day-length neutral, dense-tillering type, with very high yield potential, if grown, as intended, as part of a 'package' involving water-control and use of fertilizer. As has proved the case with many subsequent HYVs, IR8 was admired more for its yield than for its cooking properties.

What Pearse (1980) refers to as 'genetic-chemical technology' is still the main research focus within the CG System, although more recently the concept of the 'farming system' has come into greater prominence. Farming-systems research (FSR) concerns itself with questions relating to the integrated use of HYVs (and associated chemical inputs, where appropriate), new cultivation and planting practices and improved tools and equipment.

The IARCs are charged with the job of working out biological and technical inputs appropriate to conditions, needs and constraints in their spheres of operation. These spheres are defined mainly in ecological terms. The International Institute of Tropical Agriculture (IITA) in Nigeria, for example, concentrates on crop-improvement and farming-systems research appropriate to the African lowland humid tropics, i.e. the 'forest zone' of western and central Africa (it is problematic that the main site, 10 km north of Ibadan, is very marginal to this climatic zone, and more recently a 'high rainfall' outstation has been opened near Port Harcourt in south-eastern Nigeria).

In addition to 'regional' responsibilities of this sort, each IARC

Table 7 *Consultative Group on International Agricultural Research (CGIAR) units*

Institute	Research focus	Initiated
IRRI (International Rice Research Institute), Philippines	Tropical rices	1960 Ford/Rockefeller
CIMMYT (Centro Internacional de Mejoramiento de Maiz y Trigo), Mexico	Maize, wheat, other cereals	1966 (1943) Ford/Rockefeller
CIAT (Centro Internacional de Agricultura Tropical), Colombia	Cassava, beans, beef, pastures	1967 Ford/Rockefeller
IITA (International Institute of Tropical Agriculture), Nigeria	Grain legumes, roots and tubers	1968 Ford/Rockefeller
WARDA (West African Rice Development Association), Liberia	Regional co-operation in rice research	1971 West African Governments
CIP (Centro Internacional de Papa), Peru	Potatoes	1971 CGIAR
ICRISAT (International Crops Research Institute for the Semi-Arid Tropics), India	Sorghum, millet, grain legumes	1972 CGIAR
ILRAD (International Laboratory for Research on Animal Diseases), Kenya	Animal diseases	1973 CGIAR
IBPGR (International Board for Plant Genetic Resources), Italy	Genetic resource conservation	1974 CGIAR

Institute	Research focus	Initiated
ILCA (International Livestock Centre for Africa), Ethiopia	Livestock	1974 CGIAR
ICARDA (International Centre for Agricultural Research in Dry Areas), Syria	Barley, wheat, lentils, sheep, mixed farming	1976 CGIAR

Source: based on Simmonds (1979: 364–5).

has 'global' responsibility for one or more of the crops covered by the CG System. IITA, for example, is the world centre for research on yams, and IRRI takes in all tropical rice-growing regions within its purview. Understandably enough, a designated 'global' centre cannot give equal attention to the research needs of all regions growing the crop in question. Programmes for areas remote from the Centre headquarters are likely to be collaborative ventures with the 'local' IARC. Thus most rice work in West Africa is carried out not directly by IRRI, but through IITA and the West African Rice Development Association (WARDA), with inputs, advice, personnel, and co-ordination from IRRI.

Relevant innovations generated within the CG System are then offered to national and regional extension services and development authorities. Some of these are put together as 'packages' ('mini-kits') for implementation by Integrated Agricultural Development Programmes. 'Fine-tuning' to local conditions, and problems of social and political adjustment, however, are the responsibility of the implementing agencies, and of the governments of the countries in question. The CG System operates on the assumption that to a large extent biological and technological research problems are separable from political and social issues.

The CG System in West Africa comprises the following components:

1 An International Agricultural Research Centre, IITA (headquarters, Ibadan, Nigeria) initiated by the Ford and Rockefeller Foundations in 1968, and specializing in work on grain legumes,

roots and tubers, maize (in collaboration with CIMMYT) and rice (in collaboration with IRRI).

2 A number of 'outreach' programmes run by other IARCs: e.g. ICRISAT (Hyderabad, India) carries out work on sorghum and millets in the savanna zone.

3 Outstations of the Addis Ababa-based International Livestock Centre for Africa (ILCA): e.g. for work on small domestic livestock in Nigeria (cf. ILCA, 1983).

4 WARDA (headquarters in Monrovia), a regional network linked to IITA and IRRI, to serve the research needs of the rice-growing countries in West Africa.

High-yielding varieties developed by CG-System programmes are now quite widespread in West Africa. It seems probable that improved varieties of cassava, rice, maize, sorghum and sweet potato have had the greatest impact. Uptake of new planting material has been greatest in regions covered by Integrated Agricultural Development Projects.

A provisional evaluation of CG-System research for West Africa
Evaluations and criticisms of the CG System and its impact have concentrated on three principle issues: the social consequences of the new technologies, the appropriateness of the varieties themselves, and a range of institutional and organizational questions concerning, for example, delivery of inputs or the impact of the IARCs on research at the national level.

The social consequences of the Green Revolution
Griffin (1976) and Pearce (1980) have surveyed Asian and Latin American evidence that high-yielding varieties benefit richer farmers disproportionately. This is often because the varieties concerned require additional inputs (irrigation water, fertilizer, pesticides) to grow successfully. Poorer farmers cannot afford these inputs. The greatly improved output from high-yielding varieties may flood the market, so depressing local foodstuffs prices. If this happens, the poorer farmer without access to new varieties may end up worse off than before, and in danger of having to sell out to those who were able to adopt the new technology.

This set of criticisms is relevant only where Green Revolution technologies have swept all before them. There are as yet few cases in West Africa where success has been achieved on such a scale.

Pearse (1980) and Williams (1981) both note that wealthier farmers have better access to the new inputs. But in both the cases they cite (eastern Sierra Leone and northern Nigeria) the peasantry was already quite strongly differentiated into rich and poor to start with. It is less certain that CG-System inputs have added to this differentiation. Wealthier, politically well-connected farmers may find it easier to join an IADP scheme than poorer farmers, but membership dissipates rather than consolidates their wealth if they experience 'teething troubles' of the kind reported for, say, swamp-rice development in Sierra Leone (Lappia, 1980; Karimu & Richards, 1980).

The appropriateness of the improved varieties

Heavy yield has been the main (and sometimes) overriding consideration in the selection of HYVs. As noted previously (Chapter 3) many small-scale farmers prefer to minimize risks rather than maximize output. HYVs often cope less well with marginal conditions or sub-standard management than local varieties. But where CG-System varieties have been selected especially for disease- and pest-resistance and drought-tolerance – e.g. some of the IITA cassavas and cowpeas – these tend to meet with approval from risk-conscious small-holders.

It is sometimes suggested that the wide acceptance of a few pure-line varieties greatly increases the risk of damaging epidemics. Commenting in relation to the Green Revolution as a whole Simmonds (1979: 361) notes that the risks are 'obviously real', but that 'serious epidemics do not seem to have followed in the wheats' and that it has been 'hard to assess scattered reports of local increases of blast, viruses and leafhoppers in rice'. With the danger now recognized, he suggests that the correct response is to promote diversity among varieties where possible, and to favour what plant breeders term 'horizontal resistance' (the ability of a plant variety partially to withstand a range of diseases and hazards) as distinct from 'vertical resistance' (immunity to a specific pathogen).

Although CG-System varieties may combine the desirable properties of high yields and resistance to pests and disease they may still fall short of farmers' requirements in other respects. It is common for West African farmers to sum up these objections in terms of phrases like 'it has a poor taste' or 'it cooks badly'. At the outset plant breeders paid little attention to apparently trivial objections of this sort. The ethos of the Green Revolution was that the CG

System stood between runaway population increase and wide-spread starvation, and that beggars ought not to be choosers.

But experience has taught a need for greater sensitivity to farmer preferences in these matters. Two points stand out. First, much of the food (typically 50–80 per cent) produced by West African farmers is for household consumption. It is especially important, therefore, that 'improved' varieties appeal to the tastes and preferences of the farm household. Many West African food producers think first of their social obligations and only secondly in terms of market sales. Entertaining to a high standard is an important value in village life. A Sierra Leone labour co-operative, for example, is quite capable of specifying in its rule book that the group must be fed with upland rice, not a 'tasteless' or 'watery' improved variety like CP4. Swamp rices are *riz ordinaire*. Fine-quality upland rices, and rice grown without fertilizer, attract premium prices in the market place. I know one Sierra Leone farmer who carefully inspects an improved swamp rice for variants with red bran, not, as the textbooks advise (cf. Grist, 1965: 4th Edition) to rogue seed with this characteristic but to preserve it for planting purposes. This way he is able to fool unsuspecting purchasers into thinking they are buying a good-quality 'traditional' variety.

The second point is that a phrase like 'it cooks badly' is often a catch-all for a range of properties connected with storage, preparation and consumption, going well beyond subjective questions of 'taste'. Is the variety concerned well-adapted to local food processing techniques? Is it readily peeled, milled and pounded? How much water and fuel does it require in cooking? How long does it keep, prior to cooking and once cooked? Mende women claim that improved swamp rices are much less palatable than the harder 'upland' rices when served up a second time. With the right kind of rice it is possible to cut down the number of times it is necessary to cook during busy periods on the farm. Since cooking sometimes takes up to 3–4 hours per day (including the time taken to husk rice, prepare a fire and collect water) this is a factor of no small importance when labour is in short supply.

Plant breeders have frequently operated with imperfect knowledge of 'domestic' factors of this sort, or even, in some cases, of the full range of uses to which their 'improved' crop variety would be put. Early work on cassava at IITA took place apparently in ignorance of the fact that in a number of countries of western and central Africa cassava leaves are an important (and protein-rich) green vegetable. In parts of Sierra Leone the crop is grown as much for its leaves as for the tuber.

Simmonds (1979: 358) tends to make light of the evidence of inappropriate breeding objectives in CG-System programmes:

These defects were, or are being, corrected in later cycles of breeding and there is no reason to suppose they need to be a permanent feature.

Setting correct, or more appropriate, plant breeding objectives, he suggests, is largely a technical problem. One way of solving the problem is through cost-benefit analysis. Another – increasingly common in CG-System programmes – is to organize social, nutritional and 'consumer preference' surveys. There is no doubt that these are useful measures, but, as I shall later argue, they may not go far enough.

Organizational and institutional issues

Three issues stand out. What impact, beneficial or deleterious, do IARCs have on national research institutions and capacities? How are inputs delivered, and how efficient are input delivery systems? How well does CG-System research meet local needs? It will become apparent that these questions are strongly interlinked.

A major argument for the setting up of the CG System was that agricultural research at the national level throughout much of the tropical world was 'weak' (Ruttan, 1975). A 'strong' international system would provide 'scaffolding' while national capacities were being established or renovated. Some of these assumptions deserve to be questioned, and Pain (1983), for one, has done so. Elements of his argument in relation to the Sri Lankan case are applicable to some West African countries.

As noted in Chapter 1, agricultural researchers in West Africa had begun to develop an interest in intercropping, minimum tillage, run-off agriculture and the integrated use of topographic sequences (all themes of recent or current interest at IITA) during the colonial period. Although the record of national and regional research centres such as Njala and Rokupr, Moor Plantation, Umudike and Samaru, has yet to become the subject of detailed historical research, there is sufficient evidence to suggest that their subsequent contribution to themes and issues first identified in the 1930s and 1940s has been far from negligible in importance and impact, despite logistical and financial constraints. The contribution of the

Institute of Agricultural Research at Samaru (in northern Nigeria) to current knowledge concerning intercropping is a case in point.

Might more rapid and relevant results have been achieved, therefore, if the lion's share of resources needed to set up the CG System had gone instead to strengthen research capacities at the national level? Until the historians have had their say, the answer can only be a pure guess. What is clearer, perhaps, is that in a number of cases Government support for national research institutions appears to have wavered once some of the best and most productive researchers have been creamed off by the CG System.

The CG System is quite deliberately elitist. Concentrate the brightest talents in a single place, provide them with the best research facilities, free them from domestic worries and constraints, and best results will be achieved. The impressive research productivity of the CG System is an argument in favour of this approach. But there are drawbacks as well. One important consequence of concentrating available resources into a handful of IARCs is that researchers are especially remote, in geographical, and sometimes also in sociological terms, from many of the farming communities whose needs they aim to meet. Not only, as argued above, is it sometimes difficult to assess those needs, but once an innovation has been developed a complex and expensive system for input delivery is required.

Much attention is paid within the CG System to supplying national agricultural development agencies with research results, improved planting materials and information concerning recommended cultivation practices. Dissemination of research information and training is generously funded. The very success of the CG-System programmes, however, tends to divert national extension agencies from what some would argue is their most important function – solving farmers' problems (Fischer and others, 1979). The role of the extension agent, so it is suggested, is reduced to that of a 'travelling salesman' for the Green Revolution. Some go so far to suggest that the 'input package' approach is part of an elaborately conceived strategy to 'soften up' peasant farming communities for later 'penetration' by transnational seed and agri-chemical businesses (cf. George, 1976; Mooney, 1979; 1983).

Others are more inclined to argue that the real problem, especially at a time of economic recession, is the length and expense of the 'supply chain' linking an institution such as IITA to the isolated small-holder. 'Penetration' is inadequate because delivery is often expensive, inefficient and beset by logistical problems. Small-holder agriculture means large numbers of individual producers. Even in a small country like Sierra Leone (population *c*. 3 million) it is estimated that there are about 300,000 farm families. Perhaps 100,000 of these families live more than 2–3 km from any sort of motorable road (Karimu & Richards, 1980).

Reaching these farmers through IADP-type programmes is a difficult and costly process. Farm-access roads in Sierra Leone cost *c*. £5000–10,000 per kilometre. Few IADPs operate in villages off motorable roads. Few farmers can afford to borrow more than *c*. £20–30 a year to finance the purchase of inputs. Vital inputs such as seed and fertilizer are useless if not supplied on time, and yet delays are almost inevitable when roads are liable to flooding, and vehicles, spares and fuel are in short supply due to foreign exchange difficulties. Disaffection grows like mould in the rainy season when farmers are pursued for non-repayment of loans, especially when their failure to repay stems from the failure of the input package, or its failure to appear on time. Loan recovery in distant villages may cost more, in terms of transport and effort on the part of skilled staff, than the value of the amounts outstanding. The unpopularity generated by loan recovery undermines IADP staff morale. Input supply may fan the flames of local factional politics, as rival groups struggle to control access to packages and credit.

The alternative would be to go for an altogether more decentralized approach to agricultural development, with a strong and well-motivated extension service acting as catalyst for *in situ* change. This would imply a much more 'participatory' approach to agricultural research, with especial emphasis on local experimentation and problem-solving (Chapter 6). The biological gains would be much less dramatic than under the CG System as presently constituted, but decentralization would cut some of the current dilemmas of 'input package' delivery at a stroke.

As argued in earlier chapters, there is also a good case for decentralization of food-crop research in West Africa on *biological* grounds, to take account of the region's ecological diversity, relatively low population densities and unusually wide range of food crops and cultivation practices. In relation to rice, for example, Buddenhagen, an IITA rice agronomist, comments as follows:

The great reservoir of rice types in old rice cultures illustrates the vast amount of adaptation to macro and micro climates, and the diversity of their stresses, which has occurred in the plastic genus, *Oryza*...The modern trend to narrow this great genetic diversity in rice by concentrating on only one or two types of rice culture and with isolation or protection from the biological and physiological pressures of specific environments, is only now shifting to an appreciation of environmental complexity and the utility of traits earlier unrecognised...The focus then becomes the specific rice ecosystem itself... (Buddenhagen, 1978: 22–23).

After listing seven African rice-farming ecosystems Buddenhagen then adds that 'many more rice ecosystems exist in Africa' and that 'the complexities of the rice ecosystem itself should be the focus both for selection criteria and cultural management research...' (p.23). It is arguments of this sort that lie behind a newfound emphasis in CG-System programmes for 'on-farm' and 'adaptive' research (Ngambeki & Wilson, 1983; cf. Chapter 6).

It would be foolhardy to draw any definite conclusions about CG-System attempts to foster a Green Revolution in West Africa since the programme is as yet only 10–15 years old. Most agricultural experiments are tied to seasons and are not easily hurried. There is strong evidence, however, from an earlier and more 'complete' research intervention in African ecology (also designed to bring about an 'agricultural revolution') to suggest that current moves towards greater research decentralization are an important step in the right direction. This evidence, deriving from the story of colonial attempts to grapple with the hazard of trypanosomiasis, is presented in the following case-study.

Trypanosomiasis and the dream of a 'mixed farming' revolution

Trypanosomes are protozoan parasites transmitted by tsetse flies (*Glossina* spp.). The diseases caused by trypanosomes are known, generally, as the trypanosomiases. Cattle trypanosomiasis is sometimes referred to by the Zulu name for the disease, **nagana**. One form of human trypanosomiasis is commonly called 'sleeping sickness' (because of the extreme lethargy it induces in sufferers).

Commentators in the early colonial period singled out cattle trypanosomiasis as a major cause of the 'backwardness' of agriculture in tropical Africa, on the grounds that it had inhibited the spread of ox-plough cultivation and 'mixed farming' (cattle rearing and crop cultivation as an integrated operation). The absence of the plough was seen as the key limitation on farm size in Africa south of the Sahara. The importance of 'mixed farming' was that a regular supply of farmyard manure would allow farmers to cultivate land continuously. African farmers were forced into shifting cultivation, it was supposed, largely because they lacked such supplies.

Thus was born a 'model' for an African agricultural revolution centring on the dream of ridding Africa of the tsetse fly. John Ford suggests that the traveller and imperialist Richard Burton was one of the first to outline this model. In 1860 Burton wrote that 'it is difficult to conceive the purpose for which this plague was placed in a land so eminently fitted for breeding cattle and for agriculture, which without animals cannot be greatly extended, except as an exercise for human ingenuity to remove' (quoted in Ford 1971:1). The model survived for 70 years or so (until the 1940s) and provided the motivation for one of the most concentrated efforts to apply science to development problems in the history of colonial Africa.

Colonial science and the trypanosomiasis 'problem'

Early approaches to trypanosomiasis were grounded in what John Ford (1971; 1979) terms the *Pax Brittanica* theory. This held that prior to the advent of colonialism Africans had been subject to a large range of diseases, but that these were subject to natural checks and balances, one of which was that due to insecurity people rarely moved far from their homes. Those surviving a hazardous childhood might enjoy relative immunity to local pathogens. Colonialism encouraged much greater mobility. Safe from 'tribal warfare' or 'slave raiders' individuals were able to move long distances in search of new farm land and pasture, or to trade and labour. In consequence, they and their animals were exposed to a range of pathogens for which they had no immunity. According to this model, therefore, major epidemics, characteristic of the early colonial period, were an unintended consequence of 'pacification'. Science had a major role to protect African populations from these unprecedented hazards.

Ford shows that the truth was almost entirely the opposite of the assumptions of the *Pax Brittanica* model. African vulnerability to disease in the early colonial period was a consequence of the social and ecological dislocations associated with colonial *conquest*, not colonial pacification. The following are among some of the dislocative factors Ford notes. The overseas slave trade continued to depopulate some areas in the late nineteenth century. Great Power rivalry fuelled local conflicts in others. Imperial conquest disrupted local economies and put populations to flight. Ruthless exploitation of rubber, timber and ivory by the concession company system, and the press-ganging of labour for carrying these commodities to the coast, had as adverse an effect on settlement and farming in west-central Africa as military conquest did in other parts of the continent. Devastating epidemics gained their foothold among populations thus uprooted, malnourished, and dispossessed (Hartwig & Patterson, 1978; Kjekshus, 1977; Suret-Canale, 1971).

One of the worst of the epidemiological disasters associated with colonial conquest was the great rinderpest plague that swept through Africa from 1889 onwards. Infected cattle were first imported either by troops accompanying General Gordon to Khartoum or by the Italians in the occupation of Entrea. Once established, rinderpest spread rapidly through eastern and southern Africa, and then through West Africa, wiping out herds wholesale as it went. In some areas cattle mortality ran as high as 90 per cent.

Since cattle were the main form in which wealth was stored in many African societies at this time, deep social and political crises resulted from the spread of rinderpest. Where, for example, bridewealth was paid largely in cattle, loss of herds disrupted marriage systems and the complex micro-political calculations bound up in these arrangements. Where rules of social reproduction are torn up by natural disasters the consequences for settled life and stable management of the environment are enormous. Disasters of this kind, triggered or exacerbated by imperial rivalries in Africa in the late nineteenth century, caused loss of population and a retreat from the settlement frontier from which many areas are still fully to recover. In these dangerous decades epidemics such as rinderpest were responsible for the wilderness sweeping back over many previously populated and prosperous rural districts.

One of Ford's most important points is that colonial environmental and agricultural sciences first began to get grips with their subject matter at the end of a period of very unusual ecological disturbances, but instead of seeing these disturbances as unprecedented disasters contemporary observers thought them to be typical of the 'old' Africa.

Unfortunately, with very few exceptions, it was psychologically impossible for men and women concerned in imperial expansion in Africa to believe that their own actions were more often than not responsible for the manifold disasters in which they found themselves caught up. The scientists they called in to help them were as ignorant as they of the problems they had to tackle. Above all, they were compelled to act (Ford, 1971:8).

Two factors in particular were seen as imperatives to action:

1   The discovery that tsetse fly belts appeared everywhere to be expanding, threatening to engulf some of the best agricultural districts, hitherto tsetse-free.

2   The magnitude of epidemics of human trypanosomiasis in the early colonial period.

To explain these 'advances' the theory was propounded that the African was an incompetent farmer, too idle to rotate his crops and conserve soil fertility or, by correct tilling, to prevent soil erosion. Driven by their self-inflicted poverty families had to move or starve. When they left, the bush grew up and formed an environment for the tsetses...The next step in the process came when people who had fled from the infection found that there was no room in the tsetse-free lands, which had become overcrowed so that their inhabitants were now forced back to the bush...So the process went on in a never-ending and unbreakable cycle, for before long soil exhaustion followed again upon incompetent farming and another 'advance' of tsetse intervened (Ford, 1971:6–7).

The aim was to halt this cycle. If tsetses could be eliminated cattle would flourish, and their owners would be both better fed and able (with plough and manure) to farm better.

Massive outbreaks of human sleeping sickness were explained in terms of increased scope for migrants to come into contact with pathogens against which they had no natural immunity as a result of greater freedom of movement under colonial administration.

In both cases the important issue was to remove the risk of infection. The French and Belgians sought to do this by controlling trypanosomes with drugs, the British by eliminating tsetses (the difference in approach being explained by the fact that the French and Belgians were concerned mainly with the human forms of the disease in a region, west-central Africa, where cattle are relatively unimportant). Attempts were made to control the movement of migrants, to quarantine infected populations, to clear natural vegetation habitats favouring tsetses, to regulate settlement in zones of tsetse advance, and to hunt out wild animals acting as 'reservoirs' of trypanosome infection.

Many of these strategies failed. Some made the problem worse. Ford notes that the governor of Uganda, Sir Hesketh Bell, acting upon his own interpretation of the findings of the Royal Society Commission on Sleeping Sickness, in 1907 ordered the evacuation of populations from infected areas, and so 'initiated a chain of events that are still in progress and have led, among other things, to an epidemic of the same disease at Alego in the Central Nyanza province of Kenya in 1964' (p. 8).

Ford sums up his feelings as a trypanosomiasis researcher in colonial service in the 1940s as follows: 'we were feebly scratching at the surface of events we hardly knew existed, and if we achieved anything at all, it was often to exacerbate the ills of the societies we imagined ourselves to be helping' (p.8).

The trypanosomiasis problem reconsidered

Received wisdom concerning the trypanosomiasis problem in Africa began to be challenged by two sets of circumstances.

The first was that 'fly belts' were expanding in areas manifestly *not* exhausted by bad husbandry. Ford arrived at this conclusion on the basis of his work in Ankole, western Uganda, in the 1940s, and went on to investigate the histories of a number of other areas, concluding that 'the "advances" of tsetse which had been in progress throughout Tanzania in the 1930s and were in progress over most of Uganda during the 1940s could not possibly be explained by the theory of bush invasion of soils exhausted by misuse.' He adds 'having reached this conclusion, one began to ask whether eliminating tsetses would have the beneficial effects that were predicted' (p.7).

The second set of circumstances concerned a wave of epidemics of human trypanosomiasis in the 1920s and 1930s. A number of these epidemics were quite perverse from the standpoint of the *Pax Brittanica* model. Major outbreaks in northern Nigeria in the 1930s and again (though not so severely) in the 1950s, for example, developed, not in centres where migrant workers congregated, but in areas where the disease was endemic and local populations might have been expected to enjoy some degree of natural immunity.

The enormous complexity of the relationships linking tsetses, trypanosomes, and their wild-animal, domestic-animal and human hosts is well-illustrated by outbreaks of sleeping sickness along the western edge of the Jos Plateau in the 1930s. Sleeping sickness control in Nigeria was based on the assumption that the main reservoir of infection lay in the human population itself, hence the emphasis on controlling population movements into and out of affected areas, and on tsetses of the *palpalis* group (*Glossina palpalis, G. fuscipes, G. tachinoides*) feeding exclusively on humans and domestic animals. Tsetses feeding on cattle and wild animals – notably *G. morsitans* – were considered irrelevant to the control of human sleeping sickness (Figure 17). Ford develops an alternative argument 'in favour of a wild animal reservoir as the essential factor in maintaining the endemic state that has persisted in West Africa and the Congo basin over many centuries...' (p.416).

The hypothesis is put forward that *brucei*-group trypanosomes, which include strains infective to man, are transmitted to his domestic animals by species of *Glossina* that readily bite wild and domestic Bovidae, but rarely man; and that from domestic animals they are transmitted to man by *palpalis*-group vectors that seldom feed on wild animals but avidly attack man and domestic livestock (Ford, 1971: 416).

This hypothesis is then applied to the plateau epidemics of the 1930s in the following way. Warfare in the late nineteenth century and rinderpest disrupted established patterns of adjustment between people, tsetses and trypanosomes. Faced with the threat of raids and eventual conquest by the Emir of Zaria's cavalry the plateau-edge communities withdrew into their hill homelands for greater safety, thus severing contact with tsetse-infested lowlands around the headwaters of the Kaduna river (Figure 18; cf. Sharpe, 1983). Rinderpest not only destroyed cattle but also wiped out many of the wild animals serving to support tsetses in the bush. Thus at the same time as local populations retreated into the hills 'fly belts' west of the plateau were contracting as a consequence of the rinderpest.

By the 1920s the fly belts were advancing again to their former positions as wild animal numbers and cattle herds recovered from rinderpest. Fulani pastoralists resumed seasonal grazing in the area and trade routes were opened up for cattle being shipped to urban markets in the south. One of these traversed the lowland south and west of the plateau. By contrast, the farming communities of the plateau edge recovered much more slowly from the socioeconomic and political dislocations of the late nineteenth century. For at least the first three decades of the twentieth century population densities appear to have been stable or falling.

What Ford then argues is that the rapid spread of *G.morsitans* (the 'cattle' tsetse) resulting from the build up of cattle numbers outstripped the suppressive effects of the more slowly increasing human population. Cattle appear to have provided a living 'bridge' to reconnect the plateau edge peoples with sleeping-sickness

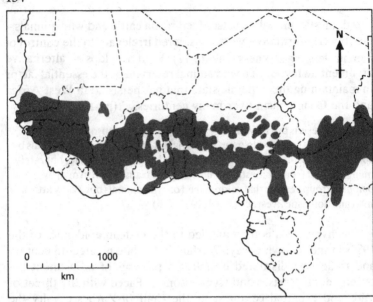

Morsitans-group tsetses (the major hazard to cattle in the savanna zone)

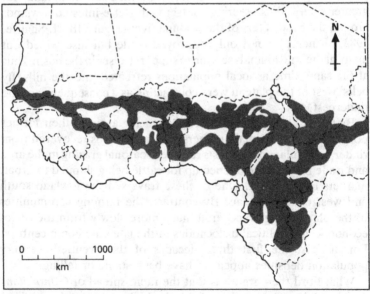

Palpalis-group tsetses (most conductive to major epidemics of human sleeping sickness)

Figure 17 Distribution of morsitans and palpalis tsetses in West Africa
Source: Ford (1971).

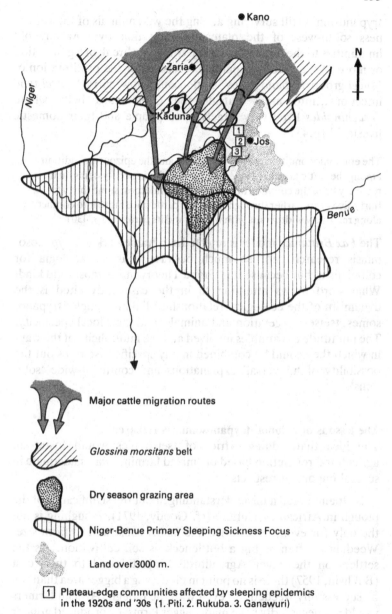

Major cattle migration routes

Glossina morsitans belt

Dry season grazing area

Niger-Benue Primary Sleeping Sickness Focus

Land over 3000 m.

1 Plateau-edge communities affected by sleeping epidemics in the 1920s and '30s (1. Piti. 2. Rukuba. 3. Ganawuri)

Figure 18 Jos sleeping sickness epidemic

trypanosomes still surviving among the wild animals of the wilderness south-west of the plateau, except that by now any old immunities to the disease had been lost after a break of a generation or more. As 'a greatly expanded reservoir for the proliferation of *brucei*-group trypanosomes' cattle could now carry '*brucei*-type infections...into areas outside the *G.morsitans* belts where *G.tachinoides* lived very largely upon people and their domestic livestock' (p.431).

The epidemic condition among the people and the epizootic condition among the cattle appeared when the two conflicting ecosystems, in their recovery from the common affliction of the rinderpest some thirty to thirty-five years earlier, brought man and cattle once more into contact along relatively wide fronts with wildlife and its parasites (p. 430).

The *Pax Brittanica* model is rejected as a framework for trypanosomiasis research, not so much because it is an apologia for colonialism, but because it is Grand Theory of the most rigid kind. What Ford draws attention to in the case-study cited is the dynamism of the ecological relationships linking people, trypanosomes, tsetses, vegetation and animals, and their local specificity. The multitude of variables involved and the multiplicity of the ways in which they could be combined in any specific case rules out the possibility of 'universal' explanations and continent-wide 'solutions'.

The lessons of colonial trypanosomiasis research
The idea that ridding Africa of tsetse flies would foster an agricultural revolution based on 'mixed farming' was inadequate in several important respects:

1   It embodied a misunderstanding about the significance of the plough in African agriculture (cf. Goody, 1971). Ploughing is not the only (or even, necessarily, the main) constraint to farm size. Weeding is often as big a bottleneck as soil cultivation. As the settlers on the Niger Agricultural Project found to their cost (Baldwin, 1957) there is no point in ploughing a bigger area than can be successfully weeded. So even with the plough, African farmers would not necessarily have made bigger farms, or produced greater surpluses.

2   African cultivators employ 'shifting cultivation' because they

have surplus land and a shortage of labour, not because they lack the means, or the knowledge of how, to manure the soil.

3   Attempts to control tsetses often had unintended and undesirable consequences, due to failure to understand the complexities of the ecological relationships involved. Ford notes that 'the relief obtained by very heavy expenditure on tsetse control is only temporary, and reduction of expenditure or relaxation of effort must be followed by catastrophic losses of cattle' (p.490).

Colonial trypanosomiasis researchers 'left...a legacy of ideas that had little relevance to the biological processes with which they had unwittingly interfered' (Ford 1971:10).

The lesson was clear in Rhodesia, where an efficient system of control had been used for many years...with some small exceptions, the main foci of tsetse infestation and of endemic human trypanosomiais have not been eliminated and the limits to which indigenous people of the country had reduced them before 1890 are still not reached. (Ford, 1971: 491).

If, in the case of trypanosomiasis research, science had little to contribute to an African agricultural revolution, what of the ordinary people? Ford notes that 'it is a curious comment to make upon the efforts of colonial scientists to control trypanosomiasis, that they almost entirely overlooked the very considerable achievements of the indigenous peoples in overcoming the obstacle of trypanosomiasis to tame and exploit the natural ecosystems of tropical Africa by cultural and physiological adjustment both in themselves and their domestic animals' (p.9).

The failure of the colonial model required that the trypansomiasis problem be rethought. Two changes were required: a greater concentration of resources and effort on a new branch of ecological science ('a systematic approach to the epidemiological consequences of ecosystem confrontation'), and a new partnership between scientists and peasant communities:

Much effort and expense might be spared if it were borne in mind that Africans, centuries ago, found solutions to the problems created by the presence of tsetses and trypanosomes. They were interrupted in the work of converting bush to cultivation and pasture by the European impact. The problem that now confronts scientists concerned with trypanosomiasis is how best to use their knowledge to facilitate and accelerate the African's task of reducing and managing the wildlife ecosystems of the continent (Ford, 1971: 493).

The Green Revolution and Grand Theory

Why was it so difficult for colonial scientists working on trypanoso-miasis to take into account 'the very considerable achievements of the indigenous peoples...'? Part of the answer lies in the widespread acceptance of a model of cultural evolution grounded in the work of Grand Theorists such as Spencer, Darwin, and Marx. The problems faced by African farmers were thought to be characteristic of a particular 'stage' in societal development. Science belonged to a later stage in this evolutionary process. It was difficult to believe, therefore, that 'backward' farmers might be in the process of work-ing out relevant answers to their own problems, or had anything worth teaching to scientists, the front runners of 'progress'.

G.B. Masefield, historian of the British colonial agricultural services, believes the following statement by Sir Charles Jeffries sums up a set of assumptions shared by the majority of agricultural officers throughout the colonial period:

The initiative, the knowledge and wealth, which alone have enabled the traditional evils of poverty, disease and ignorance to be successfully attacked have for the most part been supplied, not by those who suffered from these handicaps (for they were in no position to help themselves) but by alien authorities exercizing for the time being, domination over the less developed areas of the globe, and bringing to the people of those areas the accumulated skill and experience of many centuries of cultural evolution (quoted in Masefield, 1972: 75).

The early phase of the Green Revolution seems to have had difficulty in ridding itself of similar assumptions. The following three examples are typical of the cultural evolutionist ambience of much Green Revolution work in the late 1960s and early 1970s:

1 An IITA researcher, Buddenhagen (1978: 11), despite a generally sensitive account of the diversity of rice farming ecologies in West Africa, still insists that 'indigenous rice culture in these areas was primitive and stagnant' and that 'this generally primitive culture extends to most food crops in tropical Africa'.

2 The WARDA entry in a publicity booklet issued by CGIAR (1980: 48) asserts that in West Africa 'rice production is stagnant, changing only imperceptibly from generation to generation, while population and *per capita* consumption increase steadily'.

3 Greenland (1975), at the time Research Director at IITA, ends a valuable summary of the case for research strategy attuned to the

small-farmer with an argument influenced by the evolutionary rhetoric of the Boserup model (cf. Greenland cited in FAO/LRD 1980). Indigenous development by 'shifting cultivators' has been stalled by population pressure. Green Revolution technology will help restart the evolutionary engine. '*Evolution* to continuous cultivation will follow *naturally*' (my emphasis) from the adoption of IITA innovations.

As I argued earlier, an important difficulty with models and assumptions of this sort is that they are so awkward to test against historical data. Surprises are sometimes in store where this proves possible. It is widely assumed, for example, that fallow intervals on upland farms in Sierra Leone are declining steadily in the face of population pressure. Historical data do not support this picture. A nationwide survey (FAO/LRD, 1980) found an average fallow interval of 8.8 years in 1978. Contrary to the vague assumption that fallow intervals of perhaps 30–40 years were common a generation ago, Douglas Scotland (the first Director of Agriculture at Njala) reported 6 years as the typical fallow interval in the Njala area in 1912 (today it would be 7 or 8 years). Thomas Winterbottom, resident in Freetown 1792–6, included a chapter on farming methods in his book on Sierra Leone (Winterbottom, 1803). He reports a typical fallow interval of 4–7 years. Dapper, writing about rice farming in the Cape Mount area at the end of the seventeenth century, claims fallow intervals of 3 years, although in this case the bulk of the rice may have been grown in the run-off zone and swamps (cited in Jones, 1983).

Do we draw the surprising conclusion that fallow intervals *increased* between the late seventeenth and mid twentieth centuries? Perhaps not, on the basis of only a handful of figures. Nevertheless they do serve as a warning that the logic of a cultural evolutionist model is no substitute for evidence, and that Africa's recent past is little guide to the longer-term ecological picture because it is so difficult to see past the chaos of the rinderpest and other late nineteenth century upheavals.

There are two pitfalls of great practical importance to be noted when models of cultural evolution are pressed into service as guides to agricultural development policy:

1   That sets of features arbitrarily deemed 'ancient' or 'primitive' will be disregarded as of no further relevance, and never

properly understood, or exploited effectively for development purposes.

2   That other features, deemed 'advanced', will be introduced as the logical 'next step', without reference to the needs and interests of the farmers for whom they are intended.

The following account by Harrison (1980: 75) of a village development project in Burkina Faso (Upper Volta) springs both these traps. According to Harrison 'the introduction of irrigation was putting Ramdullah [the village in question] through Asia's earlier agricultural revolution' with a second phase just about to begin 'to take her and other villages through Europe's agricultural revolution, based on mixed farming and crop rotation'.

...the villagers of Ramdullah never cultivated this richest portion of their lands...the solution would hit any Asian farmer in the eye: irrigate in the dry season, grow rice in the wet. But the idea is as exotic to the local Mossi tribe as space travel. They have never practised these things, and do not know how to (Harrison, 1980:73).

Given the rich diversity of bottom land cultivation systems in West Africa it seems unlikely (i) that the villagers of Ramdullah are as ignorant as they are portrayed and (ii) that they would have much to gain from exotic (Asian?) techniques. A.C. Pillai's advice to the Government of Sierra Leone in 1921 might be more appropriate, namely, to recruit some local farmers expert in West African methods of valley-bottom cultivation to act as extension agents. The farming practices of one group in the vicinity with relevant agronomic expertise have been described in detail by Savonnet (1976).

The nub of the problem with cultural evolutionist models is that they confuse 'history' and 'geography'. The highly specific problems of highly specific environments, so Ford's study shows, could not be addressed effectively while scientists remained hooked on 'stage theory' interpretations of the trypanosomiasis problem. Only when the idea was abandoned that trypanosomiasis was in some way the outcome of the 'backwardness' of African agriculture, or the difficulties experienced by 'primitive' Africans in adapting to a rapidly changing 'modern' world, could local ecological management skills be appreciated for what they were worth, namely, a resource upon which new approaches to the trypanosomiasis problem might draw.

It is appropriate to conclude the present chapter, therefore, by taking note of some encouraging evidence that Green Revolution research in the 1980s is similarly about to throw off some of the conceptual constraints imposed by cultural evolutionist models. Greenland (1984), writing about rice research at IRRI, notes that the majority of improved varieties have been developed for water-controlled environments. And yet only 30 per cent of all rice hectarage in the tropics is 'irrigated land' in this strict sense. In areal terms, half the rice in the tropical zone comes from naturally-flooded land and 20 per cent from rain-fed uplands. In these areas 'subject to drought or flood or a combination of both' farmers are 'largely restricted to use of varieties able to yield little better than 1 t ha^{-1}'. Greenland argues that research addressed to the problems of rice cultivation in 'these less advantaged areas' ought now to be a priority at IRRI and other international centres.

From the populist perspective pursued in this book this is a welcome shift of emphasis. I would argue, however, that Greenland's conclusion implies more than a straightforward reorientation of 'on-site' research priorities. In the 'less advantaged areas' to which he directs attention it would be wrong to view farmers as the hapless victims of environmental circumstances beyond their control. The evidence presented in earlier chapters shows that West African farmers are especially skilful at 'riding the system'. Labour-intensive attempts to impose strict controls over farming conditions tend to be eschewed in favour of an approach in which farmers 'imitate' processes at work in the natural landscape. As pointed out on several occasions previously, this makes for great diversity of local farming practices. If the International Agricultural Research Centres are to contribute successful innovations in these kinds of circumstances they will have to pay attention to the lessons of Ford's study of the ecology of the trypanosomiases. Local ecological skills and initiatives cannot be ignored. Peasant farmers are often the *only* experts on local ecological conditions, and the problems and opportunities posed by such conditions. In consequence, the research effort must be a partnership between 'formal' science on the one hand and 'community ecological knowledge' on the other. The practical issues involved in extending this new, location-specific, ecologically-particularistic approach to West African agriculture, and rural development more generally, constitute the theme of the final chapter.

6 People's science: a Green Revolution from within?

On-farm experimentation

Despite the publicity surrounding the Green Revolution's 'miracle rices' two of the most successful improved upland rices in Sierra Leone and Liberia, ROK 3 and LAC 23, are of local provenance. LAC 23 was selected from local *sativa* populations by Dr T. Hart working in Liberia in 1967–8 and ROK 3, released by Rokupr in 1974, is derived (as farmers are quick to point out, cf. Johnny, 1979) from the variety known in Mende as **ngiyema yakei** (Virmani, Olufowote & Abifarin, 1978). This prompts the question 'might agricultural progress be that much more swift if farmer experiments, selections and preferences are an integral element of the research drive from the outset?'

In 1982 IITA sponsored a workshop on the subject of on-farm experimentation (Kirkby, 1984). Summarizing the discussion in a paper entitled 'moving research to farmers' fields' Ngambeki & Wilson (1983) comment:

> For any one of several hundred reasons – having to do with land rights, labor and other inputs, or the farmers and consumers' preferences – what succeeds under experimental conditions may not work in the farmers' fields. A growing number of agricultural research institutes, having recognized the limitations of station research alone, are establishing on-farm research programs.

The same article goes on to outline the steps to be taken in organizing agricultural experiments on this basis. The initial requirement is a set of surveys to determine the chief characteristics of the area in question, the main types of soils and farming systems, and the main constraints faced by farmers.

Once suitable farms and potential participants have been identified the experiment itself can be designed. The aim is to conduct this with the farmer's active collaboration:

The chief advantage of experimenting on farms is that, by putting researchers in touch with the farmers' views and conditions, it considerably broadens the researchers' understanding of the technical as well as social aspects of farming systems. On-farm experimentation guarantees that new ideas and techniques being channeled into rural communities are truly relevant and acceptable to the farmers and perform well under actual farm conditions (Ngambeki & Wilson, 1983).

After discussing topics such as the representativeness of farms chosen for experimentation, and selection of target groups ('relatively homogenous groups...likely to respond in a fairly uniform way to the results of the experiment'), Ngambeki & Wilson make some interesting comments about the ways in which on-farm experiments differ in research design from 'controlled experiments at research stations'.

It may...be difficult to plant at all locations within a few days and almost impossible to find farm plots of uniform soil. Other types of interference, such as pest attacks or bad weather, may affect some treatments and not others.

This is a salutory reminder of one of the reasons why 'formal' scientific research procedures on experimental stations, with the stress on controlling all variables except the one or two under direct investigation, 'miss the point' as far as many small-holders are concerned. The main concern of farmers is how to cope with these complex interactions and unscheduled events. From the scientist's point of view (particularly in relation to the need to secure clear-cut results for publication) on-farm experimentation poses a tough challenge. But sorting out 'real life' complexity is not impossible, given 'a flexible statistical design with sufficient accuracy for estimating treatment effects' (Ngambeki & Wilson, 1983: 8).

A major reason for undertaking on-farm experimentation is to secure interest, help and feedback from the farmer. But one result of this is that 'there is a good chance that the farmers will modify the experiment...'. Ngambeki & Wilson see this as a problem 'making it practically impossible to guarantee the congruence of a set of treatments over several replications'. This brings out very clearly an important contradiction inherent in this conception of on-farm experimentation: the farmer's enthusiastic involvement is sought, but in a context in which the scientist is still clearly in charge. Experiments within the experiment are not welcome.

An alternative to this 'top-down' model for the research enterprise is to explore the possibilities of genuine experimental co-operation between farmers and scientists. Before moving on to consider the potential of what is sometimes termed 'participatory research', however, it would be useful to examine peasant-farmer research capacities a little more closely.

Peasant farmer research skills: two case studies

Rice varieties in Mende agriculture

In 1942, F.A. Squire, an officer in the Sierra Leone Department of Agriculture, made a collection of Mende rice varieties from farms in Kenema, Kailahun and Kono Districts. In a preface to his notes on these rices he anticipates that some might suppose peasant farmers to be 'blind to the importance or even the existence of varieties':

Nothing could be further from the truth. There are at least fourteen and probably as many as twenty varieties well known to farmers who can recognise them at once and unerringly when shown samples. Moreover, every precaution is taken to keep the varieties pure. Seed rice is reaped from the centre of fields while the borderline between fields of different varieties is eschewed. During the drying process the *padi* is carefully rogued before the seed is put away for the next planting. Almost everybody in the native village appears to be well acquainted with the varieties and the rogueing is generally done by women and even children...All the listed varieties are well liked and widely grown and each farmer may have several fancies. Some are reputedly quick, others heavy yielders; still others most suitable for certain types of 'bush' according to individual experience...Yet the subject has received but little attention judging by the absence of records and collections (Squire, 1943).

Recent studies (Johnny, 1979; Richards, 1985) confirm the validity of Squire's comments. Knowledge of varieties is still widespread in Mende communities. These varieties are maintained through mass selection. As noted in the discussion of catenary farming techniques in Mogbuama, in Chapter 4, Mende farmers continue to add to their large stock of planting materials by selecting for useful characteristics and by experimenting with new or unfamiliar planting material. Many improved varieties released by the Department of Agriculture have been absorbed into the local planting stock and sometimes modified by selection better to suit local conditions. (This has happened in several areas with Demerara Creole, now known in Temne as **padisi**.)

Johnny (1979) and Richards (1985) both introduced new varieties to the villages where they were carrying out participant-observation studies of farming systems, in order to monitor farmers' procedures for evaluating unfamiliar planting material. Farm trials are an established part of Mende language and culture. Innes' dictionary exemplifies the word for 'experiment' (**saini**, cf. **hugo**) by the phrase **ti mbei sainiilo**, glossed as 'they tried out the rice (e.g. in a seed bed to determine whether it would grow, before full-scale sowing)' (Innes, 1969). In Johnny's case, farmers carried out (without prompting) quantitative input–output trials, using the same vessel to measure seed planted and harvested. Richards (1985) describes farmers' germination tests on rice of doubtful provenance in which the method employed is similar to the 'rag doll' method recommended in an IRRI training manual (Vo-Tong Xuan & Ross, 1976).

It must not be supposed, however, that these experiments necessarily share the same methodological assumptions or purposes as research-station experiments. Farmers may prefer the variety inherent in local planting material to the uniformity of pure line selections. Richards (1985) argues that this preference reflects peasant concern to keep open as many options as possible in the face of environmental uncertainty. Johnny (1979) and Richards (1985) both found that rather than look for 'uniform' soil conditions for a farm trial farmers deliberately sought out marginal conditions (e.g. the interzones between swamp and upland). If the trial fails in this position the farmer has the option to move up or down the slope. This emphasis on seeking out 'marginal' sites for farm experiments is an illustration at the micro-level of Ford's (1971) general point that often the essence of those African environmental management practices least well-understood by outsiders is a knowledge of how to handle environmental 'frontier' zones and ecological transitions.

Provided differences of approach of this sort are borne in mind development agencies might anticipate good results from attempts to make better use of local knowledge of plant varieties. But more work needs to be done on the ethno-botany and genetics of indigenous selection before definite proposals could be made for the incorporation of local plant-breeding skills into the work of 'formal' sector research agencies such as the International

Agricultural Research Centres. The following are two proposals of more immediate practical significance:

1   Decentralized seed multiplication. In a number of West African countries (Sierra Leone is a case in point) centralized seed multiplication has proved difficult to operate, due to a variety of logistical constraints (e.g. timely seed distribution to remote areas hampered by transport difficulties). Farmers' evident skill in handling varieties, and knowledge of selection procedures, suggests that much of this work could be reorganized on a localized, community, basis, thus cutting out the distribution problem. The range of seeds multiplied should be extended to cover the best of indigenous varieties. This would in effect be a revival of the approach of the successful 'revolving seed scheme' in Sierra Leone (1935–47).

2   Conservation of genetic resources. Some authorities have expressed concern that the widespread adoption of a narrow range of Green Revolution varieties is causing 'genetic erosion' through loss of local varieties and land races. Local planting material comprises much of the gene pool from which future improved varieties might be created. The International Agricultural Research Centres have been active in the collection and conservation of such material (e.g. a team from IITA collected nearly 400 rice varieties from Sierra Leone in the mid-1970s). Mooney (1979; 1983) suggests that 'laboratory' conservation methods are inherently vulnerable (e.g. to wars, natural disasters, and power failures). 'Living' conservation (encouraging continued planting of the widest possible range of local cultivars) would be a valuable alternative or back-up approach to the preservation of vital genetic resources. Funds channelled to local communities for work of this sort might be most useful as part of an adult education initiative covering conservation issues more generally.

The control of the Variegated Grasshopper in southern Nigeria
The Variegated Grasshopper (*Zonocerus variegatus*) is distributed throughout the forest zone and wetter savannas of west and west-central Africa (Figure 19). Hatching among the main dry-season population takes place in November and insects reach adulthood, and breed, during the latter part of the dry season. Females lay eggs during the first few weeks of the rainy season, and die shortly thereafter. Many are killed by a fungal infection

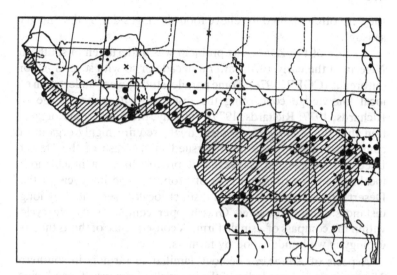

Figure 19 Distribution of *Zonocerus Variegatus* in Western Africa
Size of dot corresponds with number of records for each locality: open circles – doubtful records; crosses – unlocalized records. Hatched area indicates areas of lowland forest: riverine forest may extend well into the savanna.
Source: Page & Richards (1977).

(*Empusa grylli*) spread by dry-season showers. Others are parasitized by larvae of the fly *Blaesoxipha filipjevi*, which kill adult *Zonocerus* on emergence to pupate.

Numbers in the following year depend on the incidence of dry-season showers and the distribution of early rainy-season storms. When the rains are delayed females find it difficult to lay in hard-baked dry soil. Early rain facilitates egg laying, but the number of females may be limited by the rapid spread of *Empusa*. An explosive outbreak of *Zonocerus* is most likely in years when the grasshopper escapes attack by fly and fungus but March rainfall is higher than usual.

Adult *Zonocerus* will attack many types of vegetation, including cassava, vegetables, and some tree crops. Cassava is the crop most at risk because it takes from 12 to 18 months to mature and thus remains in the farm right through the dry season. Crops such as maize and beans planted early on moisture-retentive soils are also vulnerable. Damage to these crops is especially significant since they are often planted to relieve food shortages during the 'hungry season'.

A study of the *Zonocerus* problem was undertaken in southern Nigeria in the early 1970s, after a decade or so with several major outbreaks (COPR, 1978). Some parallel studies were undertaken of local knowledge concerning the insect and its habits (Page & Richards, 1977; Richards, 1979). Initially, there was some suggestion that the *Zonocerus* problem might require highly organized control work along the lines pursued in the case of the Desert Locust. In the event, however, it proved to be a much more localized and intermittent type of problem. The life cycle of the Desert Locust involves several distinct locales, separated by long distances. The Variegated Grasshopper completes its life cycle within the compass of a single farm. A consequence of this is that its ecology is well understood by farmers.

Aspects of *Zonocerus* ecology familiar to farmers in southern Nigeria include knowledge of the life cycle of the insect, egg-laying behaviour and typical egg-laying sites (see Chapter 4), and factors influencing mortality rates (onset of the rains, fungus infestation, parasitization by *Blaesoxipha*). Many farmers hypothesize a general correlation between rainfall irregularities and fluctuations in grasshopper numbers. In a few cases, farmers interviewed had already anticipated the main pest control recommendations of the *Zonocerus* research project, namely to mark out and dig up egg-laying sites, although these initiatives had not yet proved very successful because they had only been undertaken on an individual, not a community, basis.

The particular significance of the *Zonocerus* case is that it illustrates well the potential advantages of a research partnership between scientists and farmers (Richards, 1979). Some discoveries made by the research team were beyond the scope of farmers, because they required laboratory facilities (work on the role of chemical attractants in the formation and maintenance of egg-laying sites would be a case in point). Other pieces in the jigsaw were already in the possession of farmers before the formal research project began. It would have been a useful (and cost-effective) way of generating a list of working hypotheses if farmers' ideas and observations concerning the life cycle of the insect, egg-laying behaviour, and possible correlations between population and rainfall, had been recorded at the outset of the research. Finally, farmers had some items of useful information for which they were the main or only possible source, for example the relative significance of damage to minor, but locally significant crops (e.g. fluted pumpkin in eastern Nigeria), and oral historical information about the timing and severity of previous plagues of *Zonocerus*.

There is no mystery about the distribution of these insights. They arise from differences in the contexts within which farmers and scientists work. Scientists have what might be termed 'microscope' knowledge. Farmers are able to locate technical details in a social context. The two types of knowledge are complementary.

The recommended strategy for controlling *Zonocerus* is that egg-laying sites should be identified and marked while in use, and later dug over, thus destroying egg cases by exposure to sunlight. Few farmers would have more than two or three such sites to deal with, and the work might take a few hours. The key to a control strategy of this sort is to ensure co-ordination of effort over a sufficient area. Treating one farm but not its neighbour would have little effect. Clearing the egg-laying sites from a block of farms reduces grasshopper numbers by 70–80 per cent in the following year (Page & Richards, 1977). It is clear from this case-study that many farmers already have much of the knowledge needed to undertake such a control programme, with the addition, perhaps, of some external co-ordination by the extension services.

Informal R & D

When farming communities in West Africa work out an effective way of managing environmental resources it is sometimes suggested that this is the outcome of a long-term process of 'natural selection', as if the solutions in question had been arrived at by an almost random process of 'trial and error'. The conclusion drawn from this interpretation of invention in peasant agriculture is that indigenous techniques are well-adapted to long-term stable conditions, but are inadequate to cope with volatile conditions in the 'modern' world.

The two case-studies above suggest a different interpretation – that farmers apply their own notions of 'research and development' (R & D) in an entirely deliberate and self-aware manner, and that peasant discovery is often adequate to the challenge of new circumstances. Biggs and Clay (1981) refer to this kind of inventiveness as 'informal sector R & D', and note that some of the most successful innovations in Asian agriculture (e.g. the bamboo tube well) have had their origin in the informal sector (cf. Biggs, 1980).

Enhancing the effectiveness of informal-sector R & D is an important aspect of the populist approach to development. Two strategies – the minimal and the positive – may be envisaged (cf. Barker, Oguntoyinbo & Richards, 1977).

The minimal strategy would concentrate on maintaining a 'space' for peasant R & D by ensuring a minimum of conflict between formal and informal sector initiatives. Withdrawing the IADP-type swamp rice 'package' in favour of local swamp utilization techniques in Sierra Leone would be an example. The argument in this case would be that IADP swamp interventions are diversionary, and slow down the (previously rapid) rate of change in indigenous swamp rice farming technology (see Chapters 2–4).

The minimal strategy focuses on the notion that formal-sector research resources should be focused very specifically on those problems that farmers cannot handle adequately by themselves. This implies a very clear understanding of existing farming systems and good knowledge of local R & D trajectories, based on regularly updated field surveys (suggestions concerning the content and organization of such surveys are discussed in an Appendix). Some of the resources saved by eliminating research on problems farmers are well able to cope with on their own initiative would be re-directed to a national farming systems survey (an agency modelled, perhaps, on the lines of the national census bureau). Some of this survey work might be done in the course of of training extension agents.

The positive strategy concentrates on active complementarities between formal and informal sectors. What kinds of inputs and interventions on the part of the formal sector might best sustain or stimulate 'self-reliant' R & D in the informal sector?

One theme worth special attention might be termed 'sideways extension', i.e. formal sector assistance in spreading the best local agricultural innovations. Extension agents need to be trained to record and evaluate 'informal sector' innovations. They might then assist in the more rapid diffusion of such innovations, either by incorporating them into their own repertoire of recommendations, or by creating opportunities for farmers to exchange ideas directly (e.g. by organizing local field days and farmer workshops). The experiment tried in Sierra Leone in the 1920s of recruiting expert farmers as extension agents (in that specific instance to assist in the diffusion of mangrove swamp cultivation techniques) might be worth reviving.

A second area where the formal sector institutions could make a much more sharply-focused input concerns the question of research agenda, and identification of 'bottleneck' issues (problems that cannot be solved locally). Asking farmers to list and rank the problems they find difficulty in solving is a useful starting point (Barker *et. al.*, 1977). In all probability, however, more detailed study will be necessary to further elucidate the nature of these problems. A number of useful questionnaires have been developed by CIMMYT researchers working in east and central Africa to assist in further diagnosis of difficulties of this sort (Byerlee & Collinson, 1980).

Where time and resources permit there is little doubt that 'participant observation' (i.e. taking part directly in the farm work, preferably across a full farming season) is the best of these diagnostic tools (Johnny, 1979; Richards, 1985). Some apparently familiar problems take on an altogether new significance when seen from a participant's perspective.

Weeds on upland rice farms in Sierra Leone are a case in point. Formal sector research on rice weeds in West Africa has concentrated on the weeds which grow along with the rice (cf. Nyoka, 1981). No research has yet been done on weed growth in the upland farm between clearing and planting, despite the priority farmers assign to this issue. From the farmer's point of view this earlier phase of weed growth is especially important because it determines how easy or difficult it is to hoe the farm after the rice has been broadcast. Deep-rooting *Urena lobata* and convolvulaceous creepers such as *Ipomoea involucrans* are especially troublesome to hoe. Mogbuama farmers (Richards, 1985) reckon that the various sedges known in Mende as **togbe** are their most troublesome weeds (Table 8) once the rice has been planted.

Participatory research

Participatory research is a 'self help' concept. The basic notion is that problem definition and perhaps much of the research itself will be undertaken by appropriate 'user groups' (Hall, 1981). The role of the scientist is that of a consultant: to collaborate rather than direct. The idea seems potentially well-suited to many of the ecosystem adjustment problems characteristic of agricultural development in West Africa. The case for participatory research is based on the argument that it is an efficient way of meeting localized research needs and of mobilizing local skills and initiative. The

Table 8 *Pre- and post-ploughing weeds on rice farms in Mogbuama*

| | Farmer ranking of severity of weed infestation | |
	Rank pre-planting	Rank post-planting
Weed		
sogbe *(Urena lobata)*	1	3
ndondoko (espec. *Ipomoea involucrata*)	2	5
helo (*Sida* spp.)	3	3
ndondenguli (*Paullinia pinnata?*)	4	2
togbe (various sedges)	5	1

Source: Richards (1985)

point about 'mobilization' is that this is not just a way of acquiring useful skills 'on the cheap' but that organizing around a project which makes effective use of local skills and knowledge provides a launching pad for additional skill formation and thus improves prospects for self-reliant development (Bradley, Raynault & Torrealba, 1977; War on Want, 1980).

The kind of context in which participatory research might be expected to operate is well-illustrated by Adams' (1981) account of peasant development initiative in the valley of the River Senegal. A returning migrant to the Bakel area helped stimulate the formation of a federation of peasant development associations during the mid-1970s. These associations began to develop collective farms for maize and vegetable cultivation, drawing on the agronomic advice of a French technician. The project was funded by grants from voluntary agencies. After a successful first year, attempts were made to bring the peasant associations under the control of an agricultural development authority, SAED (the Société d'Amenagement et d'Exploitation du Delta du Fleuve Senegal). SAED, the agency in charge of the irrigated rice scheme at Richard-Toll, was in the process of extending its rice cultivation activities up-stream. The peasant associations resisted formal incorporation within SAED on the grounds that they would become indebted to the project and be required to change the emphasis of their farming activities from crops such as maize, millet and vegetables, to rice. The local subsistence crop is millet for which prices were at that time 50 per cent better than rice (a crop consumed mostly in urban areas).

Although this conflict was still unresolved when Adams wrote she notes that it had given the peasant associations a clear sense of the difference between *developpement paysan* and *developpement de fonctionnaires*:

The choice was not between innovation and stagnation, but between change evolved from within, and change imposed from without. [Peasants] had organized on their own, and had shown themselves capable of adapting to new crops and new techniques... (Adams, 1981: 341).

The SAED top-down approach to development was dominated by 'outside' interests and considerations (a concern by bureaucrats to maintain their own privileges, and overriding political concern to secure cheap and plentiful food for urban areas). Peasant concerns focused on the need to bolster local food production and to provide alternatives to labour migration. Irrigated monocropping of rice was of little interest from the peasant point of view. They much preferred the option of 'diversified, collective irrigated farming as a complement to rainy-season family-based subsistence farming: as a safeguard in years of poor rainfall...and as a source of revenue in good years...' (Adams, 1981: 351). From a technical point of view SAED objectives are not necessarily inappropriate. The problem is how to engage local interest, where peasants have their own land, and little sense of dependence on government agencies. The chairman of one of the peasant associations summed up the matter by saying 'if peasants can't profit by their own work, then they can just continue with their own farming, as before. Our grandfathers made a living out of farming; so long as we have our **daba** [hoe], no one need be in want' (Adams, 1981: 340). Participatory research comes into its own precisely in contexts such as this, where development agencies have little leverage with peasant groups short of brutal compulsion, and where local groups have worked out a clearly defined set of objectives, and have started to explore the technical and environmental constraints to achieving these objectives. The peasant associations of the Bakel area had defined the issue as one of integrating 'upland' and 'floodland' agriculture.

SAED agents were not geared up to provide this kind of advice, being constrained by their project's interest in a single crop and a single category of land (irrigated 'perimeters' along the river flood plain). Hence, there was need for a new relationship between researchers and development agency officials on the one hand and peasant groupings on the other, in which the user groups defined the problem in their own terms and commissioned 'participatory research' much as, on a national scale, governments commission research by consultants.

Successful participatory research depends on two key factors:

1 The existence of strong local organizations capable of formulating tractable problems, and of carrying out much of the necessary R & D for themselves.

2 Contact between scientist-consultants and user groups on a regular and continuing basis (this implies decentralization of research facilities, and a willingness of scientists to live and work for considerable periods under village conditions).

In some cases (e.g. the peasant associations described above) the circumstances are already propitious (except when thrown out of gear by the intervention of 'top-down' agencies such as SAED). In others, attention will have to be given to the problem of how to foster these essential pre-conditions. Some of the issues to be addressed are covered in the following notes:

1 A small-projects programme directed at community self-help groups and 'indigenous co-operatives' (e.g. savings and work groups) is a good way to foster initial links between formal and informal sectors, and to home-in on participatory research agenda. King (1981) analysing the performance of co-operatives in northern Nigeria points out that one of the problems with government-organized co-operatives is that they come as a standard package, and frequently fail to take root because there are no 'standard' villages. Indigenous co-operatives thrive because they reflect local needs and circumstances. The issue, then, is not to bundle peasants into formal-sector 'producer co-operatives', 'farmers unions' or whatever, but to seek to foster a direct link between formal sector R & D agencies and informal-sector 'self-help' groupings.

2 There are strong potential complementarities between participatory research and the process of acquiring a range of other skills. I know of cases in which farmers in eastern Sierra Leone use

indigenous **kikaku** script to keep records of farm trials. Analysing input–output trials or local market trends, or writing letters to planning agencies spelling out local needs and priorities for research assistance, might prove useful focuses for the 'problem solving' approach to adult education advocated by Freire (1972; 1978). There is also certainly much that can be done to integrate indigenous agro-ecological knowledge into science teaching syllabuses in rural schools.

3 Attempting decentralized research poses a range of practical problems relating to equipment, accommodation, analytic facilities, transport, dissemination of results and appropriate career and salary structures for scientists and extension agents prepared to work in 'non-elite' environments. The logistical problems are daunting, but not necessarily insoluble. Occam's razor (simplicity is better than complexity, all other things being equal) may be as appropriate to agricultural experiments as to medieval philosophy.

People's science and agricultural training

The idea that West African countries might pursue an agricultural revolution largely through mobilization of indigenous skills and resources has profound implications for the training of agricultural professionals. Under the concept of 'people's science' the 'agricultural expert' is replaced by the notion of an agent who is a catalyst and facilitator. Inculcating the right kind of skills and sensitivities requires a new approach to training. The following brief discussion of some of these issues makes an appropriate conclusion to the present chapter. Further suggestions for a practical 'point of entry' into the world of 'people's science' are discussed in an Appendix.

Goody (1977) has written at length about the way in which literacy transforms traditional society, laying special stress on the significance of lists, recipes and formulae, and on the emergence of the scribe and scholar as representatives of a new 'professional' class. One of his chapters is entitled 'the recipe, the formula and the experiment'. This appears to carry the implication that scientific experiments should be viewed as an extension of the healer's recipe or apothecary's formula (although, in the event, the chapter has little to say about experiments as such). Goody may be right to suggest that formulaic experiments are directly dependent on literacy. It is far from certain, however, that literacy is a similar pre-condition for the emergence of an experimental approach to agriculture. Field trials (of the kind carried out by Mende farmers) make their point on the ground, not on paper. Arthur Young, describing an eighteenth-century experiment in irrigation, put his finger on the matter at issue when noting that Mr Bakewell's 'proof pieces' brought 'complete conviction to the mind of every person who *views* them' (Mingay, 1975: 79, my emphasis).

Why then do Goody and others interested in cross-cultural studies of 'rationality' (cf. Hollis & Lukes, 1982; Horton, 1967; Wilson, 1970) pay no attention to the issue of indigenous agricultural experimentation when debating the differences and similarities between 'traditional' and 'modern' systems of thought? Perhaps the answer is to be found in what Coomaraswamy (1979) has called 'the bugbear of literacy', by which he means a consistent downgrading of oral and practical skills – as if these were in some way sub-intellectual – by those who make their own living from 'scholarship'. Formal-sector scientists are biased towards 'formulaic' approaches (so the argument would run) by virtue of their own dependence on literacy. It is not hard to locate examples of research initiatives undertaken more in response to debates in the literature than to the practical problems of farming in communities adjacent to the research station. The opposite side of this coin is the evident surprise of many agricultural researchers at the idea that small-holder farmers in Africa are active experimenters. 'This cannot be so' (I have sometimes been told) 'because the men and women concerned are illiterate'.

It can be argued that the roots of this misconception are to be found in the 'bookishness' of much agricultural education. Examinations tend to test mastery of 'formulaic' skills rather than inventiveness and problem-solving abilities. Even practical projects will tend to be assessed according to formal 'rules' of experimentation, rather than according to the test of whether the results achieved did anyone any good. This is an aspect of a very broad problem in science, which Maxwell (1984) characterizes as the pursuit of 'knowledge' rather than the pursuit of 'wisdom' (to Maxwell the defining characteristic of a true 'people's science'). Maxwell suggests that science undermines its own foundations if scientists fail to concern themselves with wider debates concerning human welfare.

Current efforts to reform syllabuses for the training of agricultural development practitioners in West Africa have already begun to address some of the issues raised by Maxwell's critique. One encouraging sign is an evident concern to emphasize social, economic and political aspects of agricultural development problems. Agriculture is both a biological and a social process. Agriculturalists need a strong grasp of both sides of this equation. A second (and crucial) area where syllabus reforms are under consideration concerns the way in which students in faculties of agriculture and agricultural colleges (many of whom will work as extension agents and in project management) are introduced to off-site conditions. There are two aspects to this. One is that students need systematic and intensive fieldwork designed to give them a first-hand experience of local farming conditions, and the other is a need for off-site practice comparable to the 'teaching practice' undertaken by education students.

In both cases the 'participatory' approach, despite the obvious problems of integrating detailed, time-consuming work of this kind with other aspects of the syllabus, ought to be given precedence over the type of fieldwork Chambers (1983) refers to as 'rural tourism' (i.e. short-term visits to demonstration farms and notable projects). One major problem with 'rural tourism' is that it tends to reinforce the strong 'roadside bias' of much of the existing literature. Villages most likely to figure in consultants' reports or textbook accounts of agricultural development are those on the main road and close to town. By virtue of their location they often tend to be untypically prosperous and populous.

The emphasis in the participatory approach is to learn by taking part. In any agricultural application it should be, in the first instance, 'learning by doing' (as distinct from the 'participant observation' practised by anthropologists which is often mainly 'learning by talking'). Work of this sort would involve sustained contact with selected farms and farmers over a long enough period to allow the student to understand village agriculture as a process. (The processual aspect often eludes the researcher confined to 'data' recorded on questionnaires or the 'events' witnessed in one-off visits.) No student should expect to be able to advise farmers on changes in their farming practices until he or she has a firm grasp of the issues from a participant's point of view. No one expects a pilot to captain a plane on the basis of textbook knowledge alone. Why should a farmer expect to 'hand over the controls' to an adviser who, in all probability, has never before piloted a farm 'for real'? Therefore, it is essential for students both to gain a feeling for a range of established farming systems and their problems, and to attempt to implement improvements (whether from textbooks or of their own devising) under village conditions in the full sceptical gaze of local agricultural opinion. Success in running on-farm trials of this sort, in partnership with representative small-holders, would be a crucial pointer to prospects for an African agricultural revolution along populist lines.

Conclusion

There is widespread agreement that problems of food production are priority issues in West Africa in the 1980s. So far, attempts to develop the food-crop production sector by 'technology transfer' have had disappointing results. The purpose of the present study has been to suggest that there are good ecological arguments for shifting the emphasis towards greater mobilization of indigenous skills and initiatives. I have emphasized two arguments in particular:

1   West Africa is a region in which low rural population densities are still quite common and where landscape and ecosystem diversity is especially great. These (interrelated) conditions pose design constraints for 'improved' farming methods not easily overcome by centralized research.

2   Local agricultural skills are under-utilized but potentially profitable resources for agricultural development. Following John Ford, I have argued that West African farmers are especially good i) at solving ecological problems of the kind that arise when human and 'wilderness' ecosystems intersect, and ii) at exploiting the risk-spreading possibilities of ecological boundaries and landscape sequences, e.g. the possibilities of combining distinct land-use elements where forest and savanna meet, or of integrating land use up and down soil catenas.

How should one proceed? Michael Johnny, having asked a villager how he thought government could best help farmers, was told 'you cannot turn a calf into a cow by plastering it with mud' (Johnny & Richards, 1981). Johnny's informant reminds us that agricultural change has to be 'organic'. Short-term applications of external aid may be worse than useless if they fail to stimulate or foster 'internal' growth and development. Biggs & Clay (1983) make a similar point when they contrast the emphasis in the last thirty years of agricultural development policy on 'dramatic modernization' with 'the slow incremental process by which Western and some developing countries' agricultural research systems evolved...'. I have argued in this book that one of the crucial lessons of the last fifty years or so of ecological research focused on African agriculture is that the 'dramatic modernization' option has a track record so poor that a return to slower and more incremental approaches must now be given serious and sustained attention. My own book, therefore, is at the opposite end of the spectrum from a recent study by Hart (1982) which forcefully advocates continued investment in 'dramatic modernization'. Significantly, in my view, it is not coincidental that Hart largely ignores the ecological literature in his analysis of agricultural change in West Africa.

What kinds of reforms might be necessary if a populist approach, grounded in the ecological arguments presented in earlier chapters, were adopted as a policy option? One area of recent debate (cf. Bates, 1981) concerns the extent to which it might be beneficial to cut back on state resources directed to 'induced technological change' in West African agriculture in favour of direct support for peasant agriculture (e.g. through price incentives). I once heard of an exasperated politician who had proposed the thesis (not entirely jokingly) that the single biggest obstacle to agricultural development in her country, from early colonial days onwards, had been the Department of Agriculture. The argument here is not just that state-sponsored agricultural research establishments and extension services fail to 'deliver the goods', but that resources to pay for these services derive from taxes – e.g. marketing board levies – on rural producers and thereby diminish the incentives for farmers to undertake their own innovations and experiments. Whereas it would be unrealistic to expect that state institutions might abolish themselves, a number of West African countries are currently considering ways of 'streamlining' agricultural support services in order to cope with large 'current account' deficits (in addition to acute 'external debt' problems). Miserable though this situation is for all concerned, it nevertheless represents something of an opportunity to experiment with 'incremental' approaches to agricultural R & D, and the 'people's science' option advocated in this book in particular.

The evidence, presented in previous chapters, of innovativeness in the peasant food-crop sector is strong, but further work is needed on the circumstances under which such innovativeness thrives, and how, in any given country, this pool of skill and initiative might be harnessed to national development objectives. Could 'informal sector R & D' be further stimulated by state support? If so, by what means? Could the division of responsibilities between 'formal-sector' and 'informal-sector' R & D be optimized? Could a national agricultural research strategy be formulated around such a division? These questions imply further careful analysis of how formal-sector and informal-sector R & D systems operate. Recent work (reviewed in Biggs & Clay, 1983) has opened up a range of issues concerning the politics of research policy, the way in which agricultural research and extension services are run as institutions, and the ways in which agricultural research aims and objectives are influenced by career and peer-group considerations (e.g. recruitment, promotion, and publication prospects). Much less is known about comparable issues on the 'informal' side of the divide, if largely because African farming has not been regarded as a 'profession' in the same way that, say, anthropologists have regarded indigenous healers (Last, 1981; Last & Chavunduka, 1985). Because ecological knowledge is often 'common knowledge' there is rarely scope for converting it into political capital in the way that Murphy (1980) argues Kpelle elders make use of ritual 'secrets'. It is possible that there are constraints and conflicts of a serious nature in village society concerning agricultural experiments and innovations, but to date the work on farmer experiments is too limited even to hazard a guess as to what these constraints might be.

It is clear, then, that any programme aiming to bring together and co-ordinate formal-sector and informal-sector agricultural R & D in West Africa will need to explore a number of these issues in greater detail. This need not be interpreted, however, as the customary academic call for 'more research'. Most agricultural extension programmes pay some attention (even if it is only lip-service) to the idea that one of their duties is to assess and report on farmers' problems. In most cases this 'reporting' function takes a back seat due to lack of funds. The first step towards a workable 'people's science' in West African agricultural development might be to take this aspect of extension work seriously and fund it accordingly. The aims would be two-fold: first to provide the formal R & D sector with data for a debate about longer-term research strategies and priorities, but second, and equally important, to provide 'in-service' training for extension staff. I have in mind a series of 'area surveys' of farmer skills, innovations, interests and problems designed to highlight the opportunities for a more participatory style of extension work. The type of survey intended is illustrated in an Appendix. The proposed programme is one that might be undertaken by an Agricultural Officer supervising the in-service training of field staff, with the aim of creating a usable base-line survey for the formulation of a subsequent 'participatory' R & D programme. Alternatively, the approach might be useful as a way of introducing students to some of the main issues involved in the populist approach to rural development.

Let me end by re-emphasizing the central point of the argument pursued in this book. Umberto Eco is credited with a definition of populism as 'spontaneous admiration for the proletariat', and to have commented that by contrast Marxists (and here he might as well have added Capitalists) 'do not believe in the spontaneity of the masses but in their organization' (quoted in Bailey, 1984). Those who share this view (cf. Watts, 1983) frequently castigate populists for their 'sentimentality' and espousal of what Hopkins (1973), in the context of the economic history of West Africa, calls the Myth of Merrie Africa. The obstacles in the way of implementation of populist approaches to agricultural development should not be underestimated. As Adams' study shows there are many powerful forces arraigned against peasant interests in this respect. There are many genuine difficulties to be solved in striking a balance between formal and informal interests in agricultural research. Factional conflict and personal rivalry are an everyday part of village life, so it would be naive to believe that self-help R & D strategies would necessarily work in a smooth and uncomplicated manner. But debating these complex and important social and political issues was not my immediate purpose in this book. My aim was to show that a peasant-focused, decentralized approach to research and development in West African agriculture is an option worth serious consideration because it is appropriate to the region's environmental circumstances. 'People's science' is worth pursuing in West Africa not out of 'spontaneous admiration' for the peasantry (though for my part I am quite ready to admit such admiration) but on the grounds that it is good science.

Appendix

Exploring people's science: an outline for an agricultural extension 'feed-back' survey

This appendix outlines a set of survey questions – arranged in the form of an annotated 'check-list' – designed to assist agricultural extension workers assess local skills and R & D priorities, and open up the possibility of 'participatory' approaches to agricultural development. The questions cover a broad range of topics, and some might be thought to lie ouside the normal range of interest and competence of agricultural development agencies. This breadth of range is deliberate, because many agricultural problems have their origin in, or consequences for, the wider fabric of village life.

Productive activities

1 *What do village people produce?*

a farm crops;

b animal products;

c produce from hunting and gathering: e.g. meat, honey, firewood, timber, medicinal ingredients, palm wine;

d manufacturing and processing: milling activities, food processing, brewing and distillation, textiles, blacksmithing, basketry, brickmaking, pottery etc. (include part-time activities for household use, as well as activities by specialist craft workers);

e services: local medical specialities, midwifery, dispute settlement, divination, ritual expertise, music, carving etc.

2 *Who produces what?*

Distinguish between major activities for men and women, and between activities which might reasonably be undertaken by each household from those requiring the services of specialists. Are there any activities which are the special province of the poor, the very young or the old, e.g. gleaning, water gathering, spinning?

3 *Access to productive resources?*

What is needed to start up each of the productive activities listed? How do individuals qualify for rights to land or hunting and gathering opportunities? Distinguish between landowners and tenants, citizens and migrants ('strangers'), men and women (can women claim land in their own right). Is land bought and sold, leased etc.? If inheritance is the main mode of access to land, is this through the father (patrilineal) or through the mother's brother (matrilineal)? Is it possible to claim land through both the father's and the mother's family?

What rules and processes govern the incorporation of migrants to the village? What degrees of 'landlessness' prevail locally? What circumstances govern landlessness: debt, refugee status, social stigmata (e.g. slave origins)?

How are craft workers and other specialists established? What kind of apprenticeship is needed (what are the fees for entry to apprenticeship and to professional guilds)? What capital resources and equipment are needed for the activities in question?

4 *What happens to the product?*

a items produced on a household subsistence basis;

b products and services entering into local exchange;

c exports to the national or international economy.

Who controls the distribution of the product, e.g. which farm crops belong to women and which to men? Which products are intended for the household as a group, which belong to individuals? What rights do dependents – youths assisting on the farm, apprentices etc. – have to a share of the proceeds? How is the harvest divided among those who have taken part? Note carefully any vested or subsidiary rights: e.g. women's rights to palm kernels after men have harvested palm bunches and processed and sold the oil.

This last point is especially important. Failure to spot crucial interdependencies at this stage can often destroy otherwise well-conceived technological initiatives. In Sierra Leone, for example, women intercrop cotton on the household upland rice farm. Cotton will grow in no other circumstances. The women use the thread to make cloth (and so, incidentally, provide useful dry-season employment for male weavers). The cloth is stored, and used on major occasions such as weddings and funerals, or to cope with the expenses of sickness or other family emergencies. To persuade male farmers to abandon upland rice farming and move to cultivate swamps (where cotton cannot be grown) has, therefore, major implications for village social security.

Local skills

The aim of this section should be to present an inventory of local skills, as a framework for identifying both untapped 'self-help' potential and and crucial skill shortages.

1 *Bio-technology*

a Describe the main farming systems for both field and tree crops, noting features such as intercropping, run-off agriculture, dry-season irrigated cultivation. Pay special attention to any features specific to the local environment – e.g. typical local crop combinations and rotations, combinations of land-use types (e.g. integrated use of hill sides and valley bottom lands), local emphasis on subsistence crops not otherwise widely known (e.g. *Digitaria* millets in West Africa), or unusual uses for otherwise well-known crops (e.g. use of cassava leaves as a vegetable).

b List local vegetation and soil-management skills. What are the major indigenous soil, vegetation and land-use categories. What techniques – e.g. fallowing, crop rotation, manuring – are used to maintain soil fertility (note any co-operative arrangements between farmers and pastoralists, e.g. grazing cattle on stubble to manure fields after harvest)? What techniques of soil and soil-moisture conservation are practised, e.g. minimum tillage, mulching, terracing, stick-bunding against erosion, run-off agriculture, heaping and ridging? Pay careful attention to the separate skills and interests of men and women farmers.

c Detail pest control techniques (e.g. intercropping to minimize pest damage, bird-scaring, fencing and trapping against rodents, storage techniques designed to minimize pest damage etc.) Are there local techniques for dealing with insect pests – e.g. local insecticidal/olfactory/fumigational techniques for dealing with mosquitos, black flies, termites etc.? Do farmers routinely identify and destroy nests and egg-laying sites of potential insect pests (e.g. Variegated Grasshoppers)? How do cattle herders keep animals free of ticks, tsetse-fly bites etc.? Are local inoculation techniques practiced, e.g. against bovine pleuropneumonia?

d Outline local uses of livestock. Who owns animals, and how are they managed? In addition to describing specialist animal production (herd management by pastoralists etc.) attention should be paid to small domestic livestock. Note use of sheep, goats, chickens, pigs (who owns them, how are they controlled, under what circumstances are they sold or slaughtered?). Are cats kept for pest control, or dogs trained for hunting or security? Are there pack animals – donkeys, camels, horses etc.? Who owns these, and how are they utilized (are they available for hire)? What veterinary expertise is available locally?

e Separate attention should be given to fishing and hunting. What techniques are employed in hunting, fishing and trapping? Distinguish widely-available techniques open to all from techniques accessible only to groups with special equipment or skills. Note any unusual activities, collection of edible insects, particularly where these activities are especially significant to the welfare of 'at risk' groups such as the very poor or nursing mothers.

f Enquire about procedures for selecting planting materials or culling animals. Are conscious attempts made to improve livestock or planting materials by selection? What characteristics are farmers and livestock owners looking for? Are such selections undertaken by specialists, or is there a widespread understanding of the principles involved? Particular groups are sometimes thought to be especially expert in making such selections, e.g. in parts of Liberia elderly women are especially knowledgeable concerning rice varieties.

g Finally, attention should be paid to the range of local food processing technologies. These include preparation of various types of cooking oil, milling grains and reduction of root crops such as cassava and yam to flour and meal. Fermentation and distillation should also be included under this heading. Over much of the savanna zone in Africa women are responsible for converting grain surpluses to beer. In the forest zone palm wine is often distilled to produce gin. Beer is often vital to mobilization of large labour groups. In Sierra Leone, rice farmers distil gin in order to raise cash to hire farm labourers.

2 Manufacturing and constructional skills

a Attention will be given to specialist crafts, both 'traditional' and 'modern': e.g. blacksmithing, carpentry, textiles (including dyeing) canoe making, pottery, leather work, bicycle and motor vehicle repair, etc. It is important not to overlook unusual manufacturing and constructional skills, e.g. well-digging, mask-carving, and the manufacture of useful implements (buckets, lamps and the like) from 'recycled' materials.

b Household skills (the kind of job every householder undertakes from time to time) should also be listed. Do people build their own houses, or employ specialists? Householders regularly undertake repair jobs (e.g. thatching) and a whole series of minor crafts (e.g. basket-weaving, spinning cotton or twine, making hunting and fishing nets) for themselves during the dry season.

c What kinds of activities are undertaken on a community basis? Community projects such as clearing paths and roadways sometimes involve very specific skills: e.g. the construction of footbridges from sticks or lianas.

d The main constructional techniques and building designs employed within the village should be listed. Who designs buildings? How readily available are raw materials? Special attention should be given to house designs and to barns. What are the good points and perceived defects of existing designs?

e Any unconventional sources of design expertise should be noted, e.g. construction of childrens' toys.

f How are the various crafts organized and skills imparted? Note details of any local craft guilds.

3 Literacy, numeracy and commercial skills

a What is the level of literacy in the village? Which groups are literate? (Enquiry should not be restricted solely to 'school-taught' systems of writing: ask about literacy in local languages using Arabic script, e.g. **ajami** in northern Nigeria, or indigenous writing systems such as **kikaku** in Sierra Leone.) What is literacy used for? Does it have negative connotations (as is sometimes the case where writing is solely the prerogative of money lenders and court clerks)?

b What levels of numerical skill prevail locally? How do farmers reckon areal units and assess yields? How are measurements made in farming, trading and building operations? What is the local system of volumetric measurement (are 'standard' measures – e.g. bushel boxes or their equivalents – widely available)? Are weight measurements employed (if so, who owns the scales)? What system of linear measurements is used by carpenters, textile craft workers, etc.? Do traders and money lenders keep written accounts?

c How is trade organized locally, and what commercial skills are involved? Are there full-time commodity dealers resident in the community? List any groups specializing in particular commodities (import–export trade often involves gender and ethnic specialization: in western Nigeria women predominate in foodstuffs trading, the Hausa monopolize the export of kola nuts to northern Nigeria, etc.). In what ways is credit organized locally (advances to farmers from commodity dealers, rotating credit societies etc.)? What kinds of co-operative groups do villagers organize/belong to, and what kinds of skills are involved in running them?

Facilities, equipment and raw materials

1 *Transport*
How does the local transport system operate? (Provide descriptions for both dry and wet seasons)? Typically, describe procedures/costs for the following five sets of circumstances: exporting farm produce, importing bulky commodities (e.g. cement, roofing materials), moving an injured person to hospital, visiting a nearby village for social purposes, journey to work (getting to the farm). Who is responsible for the construction and upkeep of the road system (including farm paths and bridges)? List the main methods for transporting loads: vehicles (type, frequency, ownership), canoes and ferries, carts, bicycles, headloading. What local 'spot improvements' have been attempted (e.g. community efforts to improve

impassable sections of road, build palm-log bridges, etc.)? What scope is there for improvements in cartage equipment (e.g. animal-drawn carts, bicycle carriers, hampers and water-tight containers for headloading)?

2 Tools, machines and household equipment
Compile an inventory of local farm tools and the household equipment of a sample of typical households. Provide notes on the adaptation of specific items of equipment to local conditions, e.g. different designs of hoe blade adapted to different soil conditions. List the major items of equipment employed by village craftsmen (bellows, kilns, mills, stills, stoves, grating and grinding equipment etc). Which are manufactured in the village and which are imported? It is especially important to take note of price trends for the non-local items. For example, village cotton-spinning in Sierra Leone is threatened by the spiralling costs of imported carding combs, and gin distillation is threatened by sharp rises in the cost of second-hand oil drums used to assemble stills.

3 Water supply
List the main water sources in the village (stream, wells, rain-water harvesting etc.). How is water obtained for cooking and drinking when farm work is undertaken (sources will often differ from those used in the village)? Is water need for any craft or food processing activities? What kinds of vessels are used for carrying and storing water? Does the village employ specialist well-diggers? Are wells privately owned, or are they village facilities? Who is responsible for their upkeep?

4 Raw materials
Note the source, cost, and trends in supply and price of raw materials used in craft and household activities, and in local construction processes. Special attention should be paid to local materials in short supply (e.g. firewood and timber for construction purposes, in highly populated savanna districts) and to price trends and the supply position for purchased commodities such as cement and roofing materials. How easy is it for local blacksmiths to obtain good quality scrap? Are there suitable alternatives for raw materials worst affected by inflation? Are there under-utilized local alternatives?

Social and political organization

1 *Organization of labour*

What is the pattern of labour inputs into farming and other major productive activities? Are there seasonal bottlenecks? How is labour recruited? How much labour is derived from which sources: the household, hired labour, apprenticeship, and labour co-operatives? Can community labour be mobilized for development projects? Under what terms is such labour recruited? What are the prevailing rates for daily labour? Note cases where tasks are specialized by gender and age (e.g. cases where young men are responsible for brushing town footpaths, or women are expected to take responsibility for weeding).

2 *Political organization*

How is the local political and administrative system organized? List relevant officials: party functionaries, local government officers, and 'traditional' leaders. Note persons who would need to be involved in any agricultural project and specify their roles.

Pay especial attention to the need to identify and consult with relevant individuals and groups outside the formal system of local government. To do this it is necessary to work out a 'map' of the major interest groups and factions within the area concerned, and to identify key spokespersons, power brokers, political patrons. Consult with as many groups as possible:

a organizations representing women and young people;

b associations of farmers, farm labourers, traders and craft workers;

c co-operatives;

d religious groupings;

e local 'descendents unions' and cultural/ethnic associations.

It should be recognized from the outset that development projects, whatever benefits they may confer, almost always damage some interests. Impoverished villages are often also intensely factional. No project has much chance of success without the active backing of one or more of these local factions. In the nature of things, however, this backing will tend to provoke the opposition of a rival faction, whatever the technical merits of the scheme. Progress will be made only by isolating this opposition, or offering the faction concerned some role in relation to the project. It is vitally important, therefore, to identify likely sources of difficulty and opposition as quickly as possible, and to invest considerable effort in the resulting process of negotiating some appropriate compromises.

3 *Local perceptions of development priorities*

I once asked an old man in a village in Sierra Leone whether he would prefer the local development project to improve the road or build a water supply. He answered by asking me a question in turn: if he were to build me a house would I prefer it to have walls or a roof? The point is obvious. Development agencies tend to fragment development. They concentrate only on what they are good at. Given the viewpoint of the old man in the village, this is no help. Those living there see a range of totally interconnected problems. By helping reveal some of this interconnectedness a survey of the kind suggested in the notes above may lead to the identification of some of the likely points at which a breakthrough might be achieved. There is little doubt, however, that some of the best guidance as to what is needed will come from villagers themselves. No opportunity should be missed to find out what people are already attempting to tackle for themselves, and what they think the next step might be.

Bibliography

Adams, A. (1981) 'The Senegal river valley', in Heyer, Roberts & Williams (1981)

Adejuyigbe, O. (1975) *Boundary problems in Western Nigeria: a geographical analysis*, Ile Ife: University of Ife Press

Adeniyi, E.O. (1973) 'Downstream impact of the Kainji dam', in A. L. Mabogunje (ed.), *Kainji: a Nigerian man-made lake, socioecononic conditions*, Ibadan: Nigerian Institute of Social and Economic Studies

Agboola, S. A. (1968) 'The introduction and spread of cassava in western Nigeria', *Nigerian Journal of Social and Economic Studies*, **8**, 369–86

Ahn, P. M. (1970) *West African soils*, Oxford: Oxford University Press

Airey, A., Binns, J. A. & Mitchell P. K. (1979) 'To integrate or...? Agricultural development in Sierra Leone', *IDS Bulletin*, **10** (4), 20–27

Ajibola Taylor, T. (1977) 'Mixed cropping as an input in the management of crop pests in tropical Africa', *African Environment*, **2 & 3**, 111–26

Allen, W. (1949) 'How much land does a man require?' *Rhodes-Livingstone Papers*, **15**, 1–23

Allen, W. (1965) *The African husbandman*, Edinburgh: Oliver & Boyd

Ambrose, W. G. (1900) 'Report on the Eastern District', *Lagos, Annual Report for the Years 1900–01*

Andrews, D. J. (1972) 'Intercropping with sorghum in Nigeria', *Experimental Agriculture*, **8**, 139–150

Atteh, D. (1980) 'Resources and decisions: peasant farmer agricultural management and its relevance for rural

174

development planning in Kwara State, Nigeria', Ph.D Thesis, University of London

Bailey, P. (1984) 'He needed to live dangerously in every sense', *The Listener*, 30th August 1984, 6–7

Baker, E. F. I. (1979) 'Mixed cropping in northern Nigeria, III, Mixtures of cereals', *Experimental Agriculture*, **15**, 41–48

Baker, E. F. I. & Yusuf, Y. (1976) 'Mixed cropping research at the Institute for Agricultural Research, Samaru, Nigeria', in Monyo, Ker & Campbell (1976)

Baldwin, K. D. S. (1957) *The Niger Agricultural Project: an experiment in African development*, Oxford: Oxford University Press

Barker, D., Oguntoyinbo, J. S., & Richards, P. (1977) 'The utility of the Nigerian peasant farmer's knowledge in the monitoring of agricultural resources', London: Monitoring and Assessment Research Centre, Chelsea College (*General Report Series, 4*)

Bates, R. H. (1981) *Markets and states in tropical Africa: the political basis of agricultural policies*, Los Angeles: University of California Press

Belshaw, D. (1979) 'Taking indigenous technology seriously: the case of intercropping techniques in East Africa', *IDS Bulletin*, **10** (2), 24–7

Bennett, J. W. (1976) *The ecological transition: cultural anthropology and human adaptation*, Oxford: Pergamon Press

Beresford, T. (1975) *We plough the fields: British farming today*, Harmondsworth: Penguin

Berry, S. S. (1975) *Cocoa, custom and socio-economic change in rural western Nigeria*, Oxford: Clarendon Press

Biggs, S.D. (1980) 'Informal R & D', *Ceres*, **13** (4), 23–6

Biggs, S. D. (1984) 'Awkward but common themes in agricultural policy', in E. J. Clay & B. B. Schaffer, *Room for manoeuvre: an exploration of public policy planning in agriculture and rural development*, London: Heinemann

Biggs, S. D. & Clay, E. J. (1981) 'Sources of innovation in agricultural technology', *World Development*, **9**

Biggs, S. D. & Clay, E. J. (1983) 'Generation and diffusion of agricultural technology: a review of theories and experiences', Geneva: ILO (*World Employment Programme Research Working Paper, 122*)

Binswanger, H. P. & Ruttan, V. W. (1978) *Induced innovation: technology, institutions and development* (eds.) Baltimore: Johns

Hopkins University Press

Bivens, J. (1984) *Project completion report: Lafia Agricultural Development Project* vol. 1, Kaduna: Agricultural Projects Monitoring, Evaluation and Planning Unit, Department of Rural Development, Federal Ministry of Agriculture

Boserup, E. (1965) *The conditions of agricultural growth*, London: George Allen & Unwin

Boserup, E. (1981) *Population and technology*, Oxford: Blackwell

Bradley, P., Raynaut, C. & Torrealba, J. (1977) *The Guidimaka Region of Mauritania: a critical analysis leading to a development project*, London: War on Want

Brockway, L. H. (1979) *Science and colonial expansion: the role of the British Royal Botanical Gardens*, London: Academic Press

Brokensha, D., Warren, D. M. & Werner, O. (1980) *Indigenous knowledge and development* (eds.), Washington: University Press of America

Buchanan, T. S., Prejean, H., Girardot, L. V., & Harris, M. F. (1956) 'Studies to determine the most economical system of rice production for Liberia', *Special Report No. 1*, Central Agricultural Experiment Station, Suakoko, Liberia

Buddenhagen, I. W. (1978) 'Rice ecosystems in Africa', in Buddenhagen, I. W. & Persley, G. J. (1978) *Rice in Africa*, London: Academic Press

Byerlee D. & Collinson M. P. (1982) *et al., Planning technologies appropriate to farmers – concepts and procedures*. Mexico: CIMMYT

CGIAR (1980) *Consultative Group on International Agricultural Research*, Washington: CGIAR Secretariat

Chambers, R. (1983) *Rural development: putting the last first*, Harlow: Longman

Compton, J. L. (1984) *The transformation of international agricultural research and development* (ed.), Boulder: Westview

Conti, A. (1979) 'Capitalist organization of production through non-capitalist relations: women's role in a pilot resettlement in Upper Volta', *Review of African Political Economy*, **15 & 16**, 75–92

Coomaraswamy, A. K. (1979) *The bugbear of literacy* (2nd edn), Bedfont, Middlesex: Perennial Books

COPR (1978) *The ecology and control of the Variegated Grasshopper (Zonocerus variegatus L.) in Nigeria,* London: Centre for Overseas Pest research

Crowder, M. (1982) *West Africa under colonial rule*, London: Hutchinson

Deighton, F. C. (1957) *Vernacular botanical vocabulary for Sierra Leone*, London: Crown Agents

Department of Agriculture (1913) *Annual report, 1912* (typescript, Njala University College Library)

Dey, J. (1981) 'Gambian women: unequal partners in rice development projects', *Journal of Development Studies*', **17**, 109–22

Diehl, L. (1981) *Smallholder farming systems with yam in the Southern Guinea Savanna of Nigeria*, Eschborn: German Agency for Technical Co-operation.

Division of Agriculture (1926) *Report on the recent attempts to establish the cultivation of cotton in Sierra Leone*, Freetown (?): Government of Sierra Leone

Dudgeon, G. C. (1911) *The agricultural and forest products of British West Africa*, London: John Murray

Ellen, R. F. (1982) *Environment, subsistence and system*, Cambridge: Cambridge University Press

FAO/LRD (1980) 'Bush fallow in Sierra Leone: an agricultural survey', Freetown: Land Resources Survey, *Technical Report, 6*

Fanon, F. (1968) *The wretched of the earth* (trans. C. Farrington), Harmondsworth: Penguin

Faulkner, O. T. & Mackie, J. R. (1933) *West African agriculture*, Cambridge: Cambridge University Press

Fischer, K. M., Muehlenberg, F., Werth, M., Krishnan, R., Schoenherr, S. & Britsch, W. (1980) *Rural development: a guideline to the concept, planning and implementation of poverty-orientated development projects*, Hamburg: Federal Ministry of Economic Co-operation

Ford, J. (1971) *The role of the trypanosomiases in African ecology*, Oxford: Clarendon Press

Ford, J. (1979) 'Ideas which have influenced attempts to solve the problems of African trypanosomiasis', *Social Science and Medicine* **13B** (4), 269–275

Forrest, T. (1981) 'Agricultural policies in Nigeria, 1900–78', in Heyer, Roberts & Williams (1981)

Freire, P. (1972) *The pedagogy of the oppressed* (trans. M. B. Ramos), Harmondsworth: Penguin

Freire, P. (1978) *Pedagogy in process: letters to Guinea-Bissau*, London: Readers and Writers Co-operative

Gallais, J. (1967) *La delta interieure du Niger: etude de geographie regionale* (2 vols.), Dakar: Institut Fondamental d'Afrique Noire

Gebrekidan, B. (1976) 'Intercropping with sorghum at Alemaya, Ethiopia', in Monyo, Ker & Campbell (1976)

George, S. (1976) *How the other half dies*, Harmondworth, Penguin

Geertz, C. (1963) *Agricultural involution: the processes of ecological change in Indonesia*, Berkeley: University of California

Glanville, R. R. (1933) *Sierra Leone: rice cultivation. Report on a visit to Ceylon and South India with proposals for Sierra Leone*, Freetown: Government Printer

Glanville, R. R. (1938) 'Rice production on swamps', *Sierra Leone Agricultural Notes*, 7

Gleave, M. B. (1977) 'Mechanisation of peasant farming: experience in Sierra Leone', *Discussion Papers in Geography*, *3*, Department of Geography, University of Salford

Goddard, A. D., Fine, J. C., & Norman, D. W. (1971) *Socio-economic study of three villages in the Sokoto close-settled zone, 1, Land and people*, Samaru, Zaria: Institute for Agricultural Research

Goldsworthy, R. (1872) 'Goldsworthy to Glover, 6/5/72', *Glover Papers*, File 5/4

Goody, J. (1980) 'Rice burning and the Green Revolution in Northern Ghana', *Journal of Development Studies*, 16, 136–155

Goody, J. (1971) *Technology, tradition and the state in Africa*, London: International African Institute

Goody, J. (1977) *The domestication of the savage mind*, Cambridge: Cambridge University Press

Green, R. H. (1983) 'Incentives, policies, participation and response: reflections on World Bank "Policies and priorities in agriculture"', *IDS Bulletin*, 14 (1)

Greenland, D. J. (1975) 'Bringing the Green Revolution to the shifting cultivator', *Science*, 190, 841–4

Greenland, D. J. (1984) 'Rice', *Biologist*, 31 (4), 219–25

Griffin, K. (1974) *The political economy of agrarian change: an essay on the Green Revolution*, London: Macmillan

Grigg, D. (1974) *The agricultural systems of the world: an evolutionary approach*, Cambridge: Cambridge University Press

Grigg, D. (1982) *The dynamics of agricultural change: the historical experience*, London: Hutchinson

Grist, D. H. (1965) *Rice* (4th edn), London: Longman

Grist, D. H. (1975) *Rice* (5th edn), London: Longman

Grove, A. T. (1951) 'Land use and soil conservation in parts of Onitsha and Owerri Provinces', *Bulletin 21*, Geological Survey of Nigeria

Gupta, A. K. (1984) Socio-ecology of land use planning in semi-arid regions. *Working Paper 525*, 1–33 Indian Institute of Management Ahmedabad

Guyer, J. I. (1980) 'Female farming and the evolution of food production patterns among the Beti of South-central Cameroon', *Africa*, **50**, 341–56

Guyer, J. I. (1982) 'Household and community in African studies', *African Studies Review*, **24**, 87–137

Gwynne-Jones, D. R. G., Mitchell, P. K., Harvey, M. E. & Swindell, K. (1978) *A new geography of Sierra Leone*, London: Longman

Lord Hailey (1938) *An African survey: a study of problems arising in Africa south of the Sahara* (ed.), London: Oxford University Press

Hall, B. L. (1981) 'Participatory research, popular knowledge and power: a personal reflection', *Convergence*, **14** (3), 6–17

Harlan, J. (1975) *Crops and man*, Madison: American Society of Agronomy and Crop Science Society of America

Harlan, J. & Pasquereau, J. (1969) '*Décrue* agriculture in Mali', *Economic Botany*, **23**, 70–74

Harris, D. R. (1980) *Human ecology in savanna environments* (ed.), London: Academic Press

Harrison, M. (1979) 'Chayanov and the Marxists', *Journal of Peasant Studies*, **7**, 1, 86–100

Harrison, P. (1980) *The Third World tomorrow*, Harmondsworth: Penguin

Harrison Church, R. J. (1974) *West Africa* (7th edn), London: Longman

Harriss, J. (1982) *Rural development: theories of peasant economy and agrarian change* (ed.), London: Hutchinson

Hart, K. (1982) *The political economy of West African agriculture*, Cambridge: Cambridge University Press

Hartwig, G. & Patterson, K. D. (1978) *Disease in African history* (eds.), Durham, NC: Duke University Press

Heyer, J., Roberts, P. & Williams, G. (1981) *Rural development in Tropical Africa* (eds), London: Macmillan

Hill, P. (1963) *The migrant cocoa farmers of southern Ghana: a study in rural capitalism*, Cambridge: Cambridge University Press

Hill, P. (1972) *Rural Hausa: a village and a setting*, Cambridge: Cambridge University Press

Hill, P. (1977) *Population, prosperity and poverty: rural Kano 1900 and 1970*, Cambridge: Cambridge University Press

Hofstadter, R. (1969) 'North America', in Ionescu & Gellner (1969)

Hogendorn, J. (1978) *Nigerian groundnut exports: origins and early development*, Zaria: Ahmadu Bello University Press

Hollis, M. & Lukes, S. (1982) *Rationality and relativism* (eds.), Oxford: Blackwell

Hopkins, A. G. (1973) *An economic history of West Africa*, London: Longman

Hopkins, B. (1974) *Forest and savanna* (2nd edn), London: Heinemann

Horton, R. (1967) 'African traditional thought and Western science', *Africa*, **37**, 50–71, 155–87

Howes, M. & Chambers, R. (1979) 'Indigenous technical knowledge: analysis, implications and issues', *IDS Bulletin*, **10** (2), 5–11

Hyden, G. (1983) *No short-cuts to progress: African development management in perspective*, London: Heinemann

Igbozurike, U. M. (1971a) Ecological balance in tropical agriculture. *Geographical Review*, **61**, 519–29

Igbozurike, U. M. (1971b) 'Against monoculture', *The Professional Geographer*, **23**, 113–17

Igbozurike, U. M. (1977 [?]) *Agriculture at the cross roads: a comment on agricultural ecology*, Ile Ife: University of Ife Press

IITA (1981) 'Alley cropping', *Annual Report for 1981*, Ibadan: International Institute of Tropical Agriculture

Ikime, O. (1969) *Niger Delta rivalry; Itsekiri-Urhobo relations and the European presence, 1884–1936*, London: Longman

ILCA (1983) 'The humid-zone programme', *Annual Report for 1983*, Addis Ababa: International Livestock Centre for Africa

Inikori, J. H. (1982) *Forced migration: the impact of the export slave trade on African societies* (ed.), London: Hutchinson

Innes, G. (1969) *A Mende–English dictionary*, Cambridge: Cambridge University Press

Ionescu, G. & Gellner, E. (1969) *Populism: its meanings and national characteristics* (eds.), London: Weidenfeld & Nicolson

Jacks, G. V. & Whyte, R. O. (1939) *The rape of the earth: a world survey of soil erosion*, London: Faber

Jackson, I. J. (1977) *Climate, water and agriculture in the tropics*, London: Longman

Jedrej, M. C. (1983) 'The growth and decline of a mechanical agriculture scheme in West Africa', *African Affairs*, **82**, 541–58

Jones, A. (1983) *From slaves to palm kernels: a history of the Galinhas country (West Africa) 1730–1890*, Wiesbaden: Steiner Verlag

Jones, G. H. (1936) *The earth goddess: a study of native farming on the West African coast*, London: Longman, Green

Johnny, M. M. P. 'Traditional farmers' perceptions of farming and farming problems in the Moyamba area', MA Thesis: University of Sierra Leone

Johnny, M. M. P. & Richards, P. (1982) 'Playing with facts: the articulation of "alternative" viewpoints in African rural development', in Kidd, R. & Colletta, N., *Tradition for development: indigenous structures and folk media in non-formal education* (eds.), Bonn: Foundation for International Development

Karban, R. & Carey, J. R. (1984), 'Induced resistance of cotton seedlings to mites', *Science*, **225**, 53, 54

Karimu, J. A. & Richards, P. (1981) 'The Northern Area Integrated Agricultural Development Project: the social and economic impact of planning for rural change in northern Sierra Leone', London: Department of Geography, School of Oriental & African Studies (*Occasional Papers, New Series, 3*)

Kassam, A. H. & Kowal, J. M. (1973) 'Productivity of crops in the savanna and rain forest zones in Nigeria', *Savanna*, **2** (1), 39–49

Kayumbo, H. Y. (1976) 'Pest control in mixed cropping systems', in Monyo, Ker & Cambell (1976)

Kerridge, E. (1967) *The agricultural revolution*, London: George Allen & Unwin

Kilson, M. (1966) *Political change in a West African state*, Cambridge, Mass: Harvard University Press

King, R. (1981) 'Co-operative policy and village development in Northern Nigeria', in Heyer, Roberts & Williams (1981)

Kirkby, R. A. (1984) *Crop improvement in eastern and southern Africa: research objectives and on-farm testing* (ed.), Ottawa: International Development Research Centre

Kjekshus, H. (1977) *Ecology, control and economic development in East African history*, London: Heinemann

Kowal, J. M. & Kassam, A. H. (1978) *Agricultural ecology of savanna: a study of West Africa* (eds.), Oxford: Clarendon Press

Kofi, T. A. (1980) 'Peasants and agrarian economic development: populist lessons for Africa', in Yansane, A. Y. (ed.), *Decolonization and dependency: problems of development of African societies*, Westport: Greenwood Press

Kula, W. (1976) *An economic theory of the feudal system: towards a model of the Polish economy 1500–1800* (trans. L. Garner), London: New Left Books

Lagemann, J. (1977) *Traditional African farming systems in eastern Nigeria*, Munich: Weltforum Verlag

Lal, R. (1977) 'Soil management systems and erosion control', in Greenland, D. J. & Lal, R. (eds.), *Soil conservation and management in the humid tropics*, Chichester: Wiley

Lal, R. (1979) 'The role of physical properties in maintaining productivity of soils in the tropics', in Lal & Greenland (1979)

Lal, R. & Greenland, D. G. (1979) *Soil physical properties and crop production in the tropics*, Chichester: Wiley

Lappia, J. N. L. (1980) 'The economics of swamp rice cultivation in the Integrated Agricultural Development Project, Eastern Region, Sierra Leone', Njala: Department of Agricultural Economics & Extension, Njala University College

Last, M. (1980) 'Conservative change', Conference on Change in Rural Hausaland, Bagauda, March 1980 (mimeo)

Last, M. (1981) 'The importance of knowing about not knowing', *Social Science & Medicine*, **15B**, 387–92

Last, M. & Chavunduka, G. (1985) *The professionalization of*

African medicine (eds.), International African Institute (forthcoming)

Lely, H. V. (1925) *The useful trees of Northern Nigeria*, London: Crown Agents for the Colonies

Lenin, V. I. (1899) *The development of capitalism in Russia*, in *The Collected Works of Lenin*, vol. 3, London: Lawrence & Wishart

Levi, J. (1976) *African agriculture: economic action and reaction in Sierra Leone* (ed.), Farnham Royal: Commonwealth Agricultural Bureaux

Ley, D. & Samuel, M. (1978) *Humanistic geography: prospects and problems* (eds.), London: Croom Helm

Linares, O. F. (1970) 'Agriculture and Diola society', in McLoughlin, P. F. (ed.), *African food production systems*, Baltimore: Johns Hopkins University Press

Linares, O. F. (1981) 'From tidal swamp to inland valley: on the social organization of wet rice cultivation among the Diola of Senegal', *Africa*, **51**, 557–95

Lady Lugard (Flora L. Shaw) (1905) *A tropical dependency*, London: Nisbet

Lynn, C. W. (1942) 'Agriculture in North Mamprussi', *Farm and Forest*, **3**.

Martin, S. (1984) 'Gender and innovation: farming, cooking and palm processing in the Ngwa region, south-eastern Nigeria', *Journal of African History*, **25**

Masefield, G. B. (1972) *A history of the colonial agricultural service*, Oxford: Clarendon Press

Maser, S. A. (1874) *Journal of journeys to countries east of Lagos in December, 1873*, CMS Archives, Birmingham, CA2/068/142

Maxwell, N. (1984) *From knowlede to wisdom*, Oxford: Blackwell

Millington, A. C. (1982) 'Soil conservation techniques for the humid tropics', *Appropriate Technology*, **9** (2), 17–18

Mingay, G. E. (1975) *Arthur Young and his times* (ed.), London: Macmillan

Monyo, J. H., Ker, A. D. R. & Campbell, M. (1976) *Intercropping in semi-arid areas* (eds.), Ottawa: International Development Research Center

Mooney, P. R. (1979) *Seeds of earth: a private or public resource?*, Ottawa: Inter-Pares

Mooney, P. R. (1983) 'The law of the seed: another development and plant genetic resources', *Development Dialogue*, **1** & **2**, 7–172

Morgan, W. B. (1955) 'Farming practice, settlement pattern and population density in south-eastern Nigeria', *Geographical Journal*, **121**, 320–333

Mortimore, M. J. (1967) 'Land and population pressure in the Kano Close-Settled Zone, northern Nigeria', *Advancement of Science*, **23**, 677–86

Mortimore, M. J. (1971) 'Population densities and systems of agricultural land use in northern Nigeria', *Nigerian Geographical Journal*, **14**, 3–15

Murphy, W. P. (1980) 'Secret knowledge as property and power in Kpelle society: elders versus youth', *Africa*, **50**, 193–207

NAFPP (1977) *A new dimension for Nigerian agriculture*, Ibadan: National Accelerated Food Production Project

Netting, R. M. (1968) *Hill farmers of Nigeria: cultural ecology of the Kofyar of the Jos Plateau*, Seattle: University of Washington Press

Ngambeki, D. S. & Wilson, G. F. (1983) 'Moving research to farmers' fields', *IITA Research Briefs* **4** (4), 1 & 7–8

Norman, D. W. (1967) *An economic study of three villages in Zaria Province, 1, Land and labour relationships*, Samaru, Zaria: Institute for Agricultural Research

Norman D. W. (1974) 'Crop mixtures under indigenous conditions in the northern part of Nigeria', *Samaru Research Bulletin*, **205**

Norton, G. H. (1975) 'Multiple cropping and pest control: an economic perspective', *Mededilingen van Rijksfaculteit Landbouw-wetenschappen te Gent*, **40**, 219–28

Nye, P. H. & Greenland, D. J. (1960) 'The soil under shifting cultivation', *Commonwealth Bureau of Soils Technical Communication 52*, Farnham Royal, Bucks: Commonwealth Agricultural Bureaux

Nyoka, G. C. (1980) 'Studies on the germination, growth and control of weeds in upland rice fields under different fallow periods in Sierra Leone', Ph.D Thesis: University of Sierra Leone

Oguntoyinbo, J. S. & Richards, P. (1978) 'Drought and the Nigerian farmer', *Journal of Arid Environments*, **1**, 165–94

Okigbo, B. & Greenland, D. J. (1976) 'Intercropping systems in tropical Africa', in Papendick, R. I., Sanchez, P. A. & Triplett, G. B. (eds.), *Multiple cropping*, Madison: American Society of Agronomy

Ormsby-Gore, W. G. A. (1926) *Report by the Hon. W. G. A. Ormsby-Gore, MP (Parliamentary Under-Secretary of State for the Colonies), on his visit to West Africa* (Cmd. 2744), London: HMSO

Otite, O. (1979) 'Rural migrants as catalysts in rural development', in Southall, A. W. (ed.), *Small urban centers in rural development in Africa*, Madison: African Studies Program, University of Wisconsin

Page, W. & Richards, P. (1977) 'Agricultural pest control by community action: the case of the variegated grasshopper in southern Nigeria', *African Environment* 2 & 3, 127–41

Pain, A. (1983) 'Agricultural research in Sri Lanka: an historical account', School of Development Studies, University of East Anglia (mimeo)

Pearce, R. D. (1982) *Turning Point in Africa*, London: Frank Cass

Pearse, A. (1980) *Seeds of plenty, seeds of want: social and economic implications of the Green Revolution*, Oxford: Clarendon Press

Pearson, S. R., Stryker, J. D., & Humphreys, C. P. (1981) *Rice in West Africa: policy and economics*, Stanford: Stanford University (eds.) Press

Richards, P. (1977) 'Ideas, environment and agricultural change: a case study from western Nigeria', Ph.D Thesis: University of London

Richards, P. (1979) 'Community environmental knowledge and African rural development', *IDS Bulletin* 10 (2), 28–36

Richards, P. (1983a) 'Farming systems and agrarian change in West Africa', *Progress in Human Geography*, 7, 1–39

Richards, P. (1983b) 'Ecological change and the politics of African land use', *African Studies Review*, 26, 1–72

Richards, P. (1985) *Rice farming and development policy in central Sierra Leone* (forthcoming)

Rodney, W. (1970) *A history of the Upper Guinea Coast, 1545–1800*, Oxford: Clarendon Press

Rogers, B. (1980) *The domestication of women: discrimination in developing societies*, London: Kogan Page

Ruthenberg, H. (1980) *Farming systems in the tropics* (3rd edn), London: Oxford University Press

Ruttan, V. W. (1975) 'Technical and institutional transfer in agricultural development', *Research Policy*, 4, 350–78

Sampson, H. C. & Crowther, E. M. (1943) 'Crop production and soil fertility problems', *The West Africa Commission 1938–39: Technical Reports* (Part 1), London: Leverhulme Trust

Saul, J. (1969) 'Africa', in Ionescu & Gellner (1969)

Savonnet, G. (1976) *Les Birifor de Diepla et sa region insulaire du rameau Lobi (Haute Volta)*, Paris: ORSTOM

Scotland, D. (1919) *Annual report for 1918*, Sierra Leone Department of Agriculture (typescript, Njala University College Library)

Scudder, T. (1980) 'River basin development and local initiative in African savanna environments', in Harris (1980)

Sharpe, B. J. (1983) 'Group formation and economic interrelations in Kauru District', Ph.D Thesis: University of London

Shenton, R. W. & Watts, M. (1979) 'Capitalism and hunger in northern Nigeria', *Review of African Political Economy*, 15 & 16, 53–62

Shepherd, A. (1981) 'Agrarian change in northern Ghana: public investment, capitalist farming and famine', in Heyer, Roberts & Williams (1981)

Simmonds, N. W. (1979) *Principles of crop improvement*, London: Longman

Spencer, D. S. C. (1974) 'The economics of traditional and semi-traditional systems of rice production in Sierra Leone', WARDA Seminar on Socioeconomic Aspects of Rice Production in Sierra Leone, April, 1974 (mimeo)

Spencer, D. S. C. (1975) *The economics of rice production in Sierra Leone, i, Upland rice*, Njala: Department of Agricultural Economics and Extension, Njala University College

Spitzer, L. (1975) *The Creoles of Sierra Leone: responses to colonialism, 1870–1945*, Ile Ife: University of Ife Press

Squire, F. A. (1943) 'Notes on Mende rice varieties', *Sierra Leone Agricultural Notes*, 10

Stamp, L. D. (1938) 'Land utilization and soil erosion in Nigeria',

Geographical Review, **28**, 32–45

Starkey, P. H. (1981) *Farming with work-oxen in Sierra Leone*, Freetown: Government Printer

Steiner, K. G. (1982) *Intercropping in tropical smallholder agriculture with special reference to West Africa*, Eschborn: Deutsche Gesellschaft fur Technische Zusammenarbeit (GTZ)

Stern, P. (1980) *Small-scale irrigation: a manual of low-cost water technology*, London: Intermediate Technology Publications

Stock, R. (1977) 'The impact of the decline of the Hadejia river floods in Hadejia Emirate', in van Apeldoorn, J. G. (ed.), *The aftermath of the 1972–74 drought in Nigeria*, Zaria: Centre for Social and Economic Research, Ahmadu Bello University

Suret-Canale, J. (1971) *French colonialism in tropical Africa, 1900–1945* (trans. Till Gottheimer), London: Heinemann

Trapnell, G. G. (1943) *The soils, vegetation and agricultural systems of north-eastern Rhodesia*, Lusaka: Government Printer

Trouse, A. C. (1979) 'Soil physical characteristics and root growth', in Lal & Greenland (1979)

Underhill, H. W. (1984) *Small-scale irrigation in Africa in the context of rural development*, Rome: FAO

Uzozie, L. C. (1979) 'Tradition and change in Igbo food-crop production systems: a geographical appraisal', Ph.D Thesis: University of London

van Vuure, W., Odell, R. T. & Sutton, P. M. (1972) 'Soil survey of the Njala area, Sierra Leone', Njala: Njala University College Bulletin No. 3

Virmani, S. S., Olufowote, J. O., & Abifarin, A. O. (1978) 'Rice improvement in tropical anglophone Africa', in Buddenhagen, I. W. & Persley, G. J. (eds.), *Rice in Africa*, London: Academic Press

Vo-Tong Xuan & Ross, V. E. (1976) *Training manual for rice production*, Los Banos: IRRI

Waldock, E. A., Capstick, E. S. & Browning, A. J. (1951) *Soil conservation and land use in Sierra Leone*, Freetown: Government Printer

Walicki, A. (1969) 'Russia', in Ionescu & Gellner (1969)

War on Want/Mauritanian Ministry of Rural Development (1980)

Projet de developpement agricole du Guidimaka: rapport d'Activities et de Recherches Hivernage 1979 et Saison de Maraichage 1979–80, London: War on Want

Warren, D. M. (1984) 'Linking scientific and indigenous agricultural systems', in Compton (1984)

Watts, M. (1983a) *Silent violence: Food, famine and peasantry in northern Nigeria*, Berkeley: University of California Press

Watts, M. (1983b) 'Populism and the politics of African land use', *African Studies Review*, **26**, 73–83

White, J. (1981) *Central administration in Nigeria, 1914–1948: the problem of polarity*, Dublin: Irish Academic Press

Williams, G. (1976) 'Taking the part of peasants: rural development in Nigeria and Tanzania', in Gutkind, P. W. & Wallerstein, I. (eds.), *The political economy of contemporary Africa*, Beverly Hills: Sage

Williams, G. (1981) 'The World Bank and the peasant problem', in Heyer, Roberts & Williams (1981)

Wilkinson, R. (1973) *Poverty and progress: an ecological perspective on economic development*, London: University Paperbacks

Wilson, B. R. (1970) *Rationality*, (ed.) Oxford: Blackwell

Winterbottom, T. (1803) *An account of the native Africans in the neighbourhood of Sierra Leone to which is added an account of the present state of medicine among them*, London: C. Whittingham

World Bank (1975) *Sector policy paper on rural development*, Washington: World Bank

Worsley, P. (1969) 'The concept of populism', in Ionescu & Gellner (1969)

Zachariah, K. C. & Condé, J. (1981) *Migration in West Africa: demographic aspects*, New York: Oxford University Press

Index

Printed in the United States
by Baker & Taylor Publisher Services